Y0-BDI-532

DRAMA CLASSICS

The Drama Classics series aims to offer the world's greatest plays in affordable paperback editions for students, actors and theatregoers. The hallmarks of the series are accessible introductions, uncluttered texts and an overall theatrical perspective.

Given that readers may be encountering a particular play for the first time, the introduction seeks to fill in the theatrical/historical background and to outline the chief themes rather than concentrate on interpretational and textual analysis. Similarly the play-texts themselves are free of footnotes and other interpolations: instead there is an end-glossary of 'difficult' words and phrases.

The texts of the English-language plays in the series have been prepared taking full account of all existing scholarship. The foreign-language plays have been newly translated into a modern English that is both actable and accurate: many of the translators regularly have their work staged professionally.

Edited until his early death by Kenneth McLeish, the Drama Classics series continues with his aim of providing a first-class library of dramatic literature representing the best of world theatre.

Associate editors:
Professor Trevor R. Griffiths
Professor in Humanities, University of Exeter
Dr Colin Counsell
Senior Lecturer in Theatre Studies and Performing Arts

DRAMA CLASSICS *the first hundred*

The Alchemist
All for Love
Andromache
Antigone
Bacchae
Bartholomew Fair
The Beaux Stratagem
The Beggar's Opera
Birds
Blood Wedding
The Changeling
A Chaste Maid in
    Cheapside
The Cherry Orchard
Children of the Sun
El Cid
The Country Wife
The Dance of Death
The Devil is an Ass
Doctor Faustus
A Doll's House
Don Juan
The Duchess of Malfi
Edward II
Electra (Euripides)
Electra (Sophocles)
An Enemy of the People
Everyman
The Father
Faust
A Flea in her Ear
Frogs
Fuente Ovejuna
The Game of Love
    and Chance
Ghosts
The Government
    Inspector
Hecuba
Hedda Gabler
The House of Bernarda
    Alba

The Hypochondriac
The Importance of
    Being Earnest
An Ideal Husband
An Italian Straw Hat
Ivanov
The Jew of Malta
The Knight of the
    Burning Pestle
The Lady from the Sea
The Learned Ladies
Lady Windermere's Fan
Life is a Dream
London Assurance
Lulu
Lysistrata
The Malcontent
The Man of Mode
The Marriage of Figaro
Mary Stuart
The Master Builder
Medea
The Misanthrope
The Miser
Miss Julie
A Month in the
    Country
Oedipus
The Oresteia
Peer Gynt
Phedra
The Playboy of the
    Western World
The Recruiting Officer
The Revenger's
    Tragedy
The Rivals
La Ronde
Rosmersholm
The Rover
Scapino
The School for Scandal

The Seagull
The Servant of Two
    Masters
She Stoops to Conquer
The Shoemakers'
    Holiday
Six Characters in
    Search of an
    Author
The Spanish Tragedy
Spring Awakening
Summerfolk
Tartuffe
Three Sisters
'Tis Pity She's a Whore
Too Clever by Half
Ubu
Uncle Vanya
Volpone
The Way of the World
The White Devil
The Widowing of Mrs
    Holroyd
The Wild Duck
A Woman Killed with
    Kindness
A Woman of No
    Importance
Women Beware Women
Women of Troy
Woyzeck
Yerma

*The publishers welcome
suggestions for further titles*

DRAMA CLASSICS

AN ENEMY OF THE PEOPLE

by

Henrik Ibsen

translated and introduced by Stephen Mulrine

NICK HERN BOOKS

London

www.nickhernbooks.co.uk

A Drama Classic

An Enemy of the People first published in Great Britain in this translation as a paperback original in 2011 by Nick Hern Books, 14 Larden Road, London W3 7ST

Copyright in the introduction © 2011 Nick Hern Books
Copyright in this translation © 2011 Stephen Mulrine

Stephen Mulrine has asserted his moral right to be identified as the translator of this work.

Typeset by Nick Hern Books, London
Printed by Mimeo Ltd, Huntingdon, Cambridgeshire PE29 6XX

A CIP catalogue record for this book is available from the British Library

ISBN   978 1 84842 159 2

CAUTION   All rights whatsoever in this play are strictly reserved. Requests to reproduce the text in whole or in part should be addressed to the publisher.

Amateur Performing Rights   Applications for performance, including readings and excerpts, by amateur and stock companies in the English language throughout the world should be addressed to the Performing Rights Manager, Nick Hern Books, 14 Larden Road, London W3 7ST, *tel* +44 (0)20 8749 4953, *e-mail* info@nickhernbooks.demon.co.uk, except as follows:

Australia: Dominie Drama, 8 Cross Street, Brookvale 2100, *fax* (2) 9938 8695, *e-mail* drama@dominie.com.au

New Zealand: Play Bureau, PO Box 420, New Plymouth, *fax* (6)753 2150, *e-mail* play.bureau.nz@xtra.co.nz

South Africa: DALRO (pty) Ltd, PO Box 31627, 2017 Braamfontein, *tel* (11) 712 8000, *fax* (11) 403 9094, *e-mail* theatricals@dalro.co.za

Professional Performing Rights   Applications for performance by professionals in any medium and in any language throughout the world should be addressed to Alan Brodie Representation Ltd, Paddock Suite, The Courtyard, 55a Charterhouse Street, London EC1M 6HA, *fax* +44 (0)20 7183 7999, www.alanbrodie.com

No performance of any kind may be given unless a licence has been obtained. Applications should be made before rehearsals begin. Publication of this play does not necessarily indicate its availability for performance.

MIX
Paper from
responsible sources
FSC® C019549

Introduction

Henrik Ibsen (1828–1906)

Henrik Ibsen was born on 20 March 1828 in Skien, a small town to the south of Kristiania (modern Oslo), into a prosperous middle-class family. His mother, Marichen, took a lively interest in the arts, and Ibsen was introduced to the theatre at an early age. When he was six, however, his father's business failed, and Ibsen's childhood was spent in relative poverty, until he was forced to leave school and find employment as an apprentice pharmacist in Grimstad. In 1846, an affair with a housemaid ten years his senior produced an illegitimate son, whose upbringing Ibsen had to pay for until the boy was in his teens, though he saw nothing of him. Ibsen's family relationships in general were not happy, and after the age of twenty-two he never saw either of his parents again, and kept in touch with them only through his sister Hedvig's letters.

While still working as a pharmacist, Ibsen was studying for university, in pursuit of a vague ambition to become a doctor. He failed the entrance examination, however, and at the age of twenty launched his literary career with the publication in 1850 of a verse play, *Catiline*, which sold a mere fifty copies, having already been rejected by the Danish Theatre in Kristiania. Drama in Norwegian, as opposed to Swedish and Danish, was virtually non-existent at this time, and the low status of the language reflected Norway's own position, as a province of Denmark, for most of the preceding five centuries. Kristiania, the capital, was one of

Europe's smallest, with fewer than 30,000 inhabitants, and communications were primitive.

However, change, as far as the theatre was concerned, was already under way, and Ibsen and his younger contemporary Bjørnson were among the prime movers. Another was the internationally famous violinist, Ole Bull, who founded a Norwegian-language theatre in his hometown of Bergen, and in 1851 invited Ibsen to become its first resident dramatist, with a commitment to write one play each year, to be premiered on January 2nd, the anniversary of the theatre's founding.

During his time at Bergen, Ibsen wrote five plays, mainly historical in content: *St John's Night*, a comedy which he later disowned, loosely based on *A Midsummer Night's Dream*; *The Warrior's Barrow*, a reworking of a one-act verse play first staged in Kristiania; *Lady Inger of Østråt*, a five-act drama set in sixteenth-century Trondheim, on the theme of Norwegian independence; *The Feast at Solhaug*, which went on to be commercially published; and a romantic drama, *Olaf Liljekrans* (1857), to complete his contractual obligations in Bergen.

Ibsen had meanwhile met his future wife, Suzannah Thoresen, and the offer of a post as artistic director of the newly created Norwegian Theatre in Kristiania must have been very welcome. Ibsen took up his post in September 1857, with a specific remit to compete for audiences with the long-established Danish Theatre in Kristiania. A successful first season was accordingly crucial, and his own new play, *The Vikings at Helgeland*, set in tenth-century Norway, and based on material drawn from the Norse sagas, was an important contribution. By 1861, however, the Danish Theatre was clearly winning the battle, in part by extending its Norwegian repertoire, and Ibsen's theatre was forced to close, in the summer of 1862.

Now unemployed, Ibsen successfully applied for a government grant to collect folk tales in the Norwegian hinterland. During this period he also wrote *Love's Comedy*, a verse play on the theme of modern marriage, and a five-act historical drama, *The Pretenders*, now regarded as his first major play, premiered at the Kristiania Theatre in January 1864, under Ibsen's own direction. A few months later, financed by another government grant, Ibsen left Norway for Copenhagen on 2 April 1864, beginning a journey that would take him on to Rome, and international recognition.

Brand, the first fruit of Ibsen's self-imposed exile, sees him abandoning historical themes, and drawing on his own experience more directly, basing his uncompromising hero on a fanatical priest who had led a religious revival in Ibsen's hometown of Skien in the 1850s. Like all of Ibsen's plays, *Brand* was published before it was staged, in March 1866, only receiving its first full performance almost twenty years later, in 1885 at the Nya Theatre in Stockholm, though it seems clear that like *Peer Gynt*, his next play, *Brand* was intended to be read, rather than acted.

Ibsen wrote *Peer Gynt* in Rome, Ischia and Sorrento, through the summer of 1867, using material from Asbjørnsen's recently published *Norwegian Folktales*, as well as the darker corners of his own life, but the end result is regarded as containing some of his finest dramatic writing, with the irrepressible Peer at the other end of the moral spectrum from Brand, a typical example of Ibsen's fondness for opposites or antitheses in his dramatic work.

The following spring, Ibsen left Rome for Berchtesgaden in the Bavarian Alps to work on a new play, *The League of Youth*, which was premiered at the Kristiania Theatre in October 1869, and attracted some hostility for its satirical portrayal of contemporary politicians. A few weeks later, Ibsen travelled to Egypt, to represent his country at the official opening of the Suez Canal.

On his return, Ibsen began work on what he regarded as his greatest achievement, the mammoth ten-act *Emperor and Galilean*, dramatising the conflict between Christianity and paganism through the life of Julian the Apostate. Published in Copenhagen in October 1873, to critical acclaim, the play nonetheless had to wait over a century before it was staged in full, an eight-hour marathon in Oslo in 1987.

By this time, Ibsen's fame had brought him tempting offers to return to Norway, as well as recognition at the highest level in the award of the Order of St Olaf. However, apart from a brief sojourn in Kristiania in the summer of 1874, he remained in Germany, moving from Dresden to Munich the following year, to commence writing *Pillars of the Community*, completed in 1877, the first in a series of 'social problem' plays, although its large cast requirements make it nowadays something of a theatrical rarity. By contrast, his next play, *A Doll's House*, has seldom been absent from the stage since its Copenhagen premiere in December 1879, and the challenge it offers to male hypocrisy and so-called 'family values' has ensured its continuing popularity.

In Ibsen's characteristic manner, *Ghosts* in effect is the obverse of *A Doll's House*. Whereas in the latter play Nora flees the family home, in *Ghosts* Ibsen shows the tragic consequences of a wife's failure to break free from a disastrous marriage. Its exposure of taboo subjects like venereal disease, however, still retains the power to shock, and it was at first rejected by all Ibsen's preferred theatres. After publication in 1881, almost two years elapsed before *Ghosts* was staged in Scandinavia, the world premiere having already taken place in Chicago, in May 1882.

Ibsen was angered by his countrymen's reception of *Ghosts*, especially the hostility shown it by the so-called liberal press, and *An Enemy of the People*, published in November 1882, is to a large extent a vehicle for that anger, as well as for Ibsen's sceptical views on democracy. Ibsen's rooted mistrust of 'big government' and his contempt for the party system are channelled into the delineation of familiar stereotypes: self-serving professional politicians; spineless fence-straddling 'moderates'; venal and unprincipled hacks. Raised up against these, however, Dr Stockmann's individual voice is rendered effectively impotent by his own political naivety, a device which rescues the play from becoming a tract. *An Enemy of the People*, as Ibsen no doubt intended, offended liberals and conservatives alike, but not enough to impede its staging. Premiered in Kristiania in January 1883, it received mixed reviews.

The initial reaction to *The Wild Duck*, published in November of the following year, was largely one of bewilderment, although it was produced without delay in all the major Scandinavian venues. While the 'original sin' of the drama, the housemaid made pregnant by her master and married off to a convenient dupe, echoes that of *Ghosts*, Ibsen's use of symbolism appeared to sit uneasily with the naturalistic dialogue, and indeed still troubles modern audiences.

However, Ibsen was moving away from the concerns of the 'problem play' towards a more personal, oblique utterance, and the controversy which dogged his work scarcely lessened with the publication of *Rosmersholm*, in November 1886, following a brief return to Norway after an eleven-year absence. Partly inspired by Ibsen's disillusionment with Norwegian politics, it is especially noteworthy for the creation of Rebecca West, one of his most compelling characters, though its witches' brew of ingredients caused something of a scandal.

Ibsen's reputation was by now unassailable, however, and in Germany particularly the innovative productions of the Saxe-Meiningen company had won him an eager following. In England, the enthusiasm of Edmund Gosse, and later William Archer, ensured that several of his plays were at least available in print in translation, but the first significant staging of his work in London had to wait until June 1889, with the Novelty Theatre production of *A Doll's House*.

Meanwhile, *The Lady from the Sea* fared well enough at the box office, with simultaneous premieres in Kristiania and Weimar, on 12 February 1889, though again its complex amalgam of dreamy symbolism, evolutionary theory, and the daily routine of the Wangel household in northern Norway tended to confuse audiences, and is still something of an obstacle to production.

Hedda Gabler, premiered in Munich at the Residenztheater in January 1891, is now Ibsen's most popular play, but attracted fierce criticism in its day, largely on account of the character of Hedda herself. Arguably Ibsen's finest creation, Hedda's contempt for the sacred roles of wife and mother seemed the more offensive in that Ibsen provided no explanation for it, no inherited moral taint, and she continues to unnerve us even today, like a glimpse into the abyss.

In that same year, there were no fewer than five London productions of Ibsen plays, including *Hedda Gabler*, and the publication of George Bernard Shaw's seminal critique, *The Quintessence of Ibsenism*, helped assure his place in the permanent English repertoire. Ibsen himself finally returned to Norway in July, a national hero, though he suffered the indignity of hearing his achievement disparaged by the rising young novelist Knut Hamsun at a public lecture in October.

In his declining years, Ibsen increasingly sought the company of young female admirers, and his relationships with Emilie Bardach, Helene Raff, and finally Hildur Andersen, find their way into his later plays, notably *The Master Builder*, in which Ibsen also revisits the theme of self, which had inspired his early masterpieces, *Brand* and *Peer Gynt*. The burden of fame, the generational conflict between age and youth, and Ibsen's personal concerns are all explored in the relationship between the successful middle-aged architect Solness and the twenty-something 'free spirit' Hilde Wangel. Although the all-pervasive tower metaphor puzzled some critics, given that Freud had still to explain such things, the play was an instant success, going on from its premiere in Berlin in January 1893 to productions in Scandinavia, Paris, Chicago and London within the year.

Ibsen's next play, *Little Eyolf* – despite having the distinction of a public reading in English, at the Haymarket Theatre in December 1893, even before it was published in Copenhagen – has enjoyed little success on the stage, where its mixed modes of realism and symbolism can fail to blend, with unintentionally comic results. However, *John Gabriel Borkman*, published three years later, and premiered in Helsinki in January 1897, achieves in prose the poetic grandeur of *Brand*. The play is drawn in part from Ibsen's own experience of humiliating dependency, in the wake of his father's bankruptcy, and explores Ibsen's cherished themes: the corrupting influence of materialism, the freedom of the individual, self-doubt, and marital disharmony.

Ibsen was now permanently resident in Kristiania, venerated wherever he went, and his seventieth birthday, on 20 March 1898, was the occasion for widespread rejoicing. His collected works were in preparation in both Denmark and Germany, and his international fame rivalled that of Tolstoy. It is fitting, therefore, that Ibsen's last play, *When We Dead Awaken*, should have been premiered on 15 January 1900, in effect launching the next century, at Kristiania's new National Theatre, the confident expression of that Norwegian identity which Ibsen and Bjørnson, whose statues graced its entrance, did so much to promote.

Finally, like almost all of Ibsen's plays, *When We Dead Awaken* is a response to the author's psychic needs, and it can be argued that the ageing sculptor Rubek's return to his first inspiration, Irene, now confined in a sanatorium, hints at Ibsen's feelings of guilt over his neglect of his wife Suzannah, and his belated recognition that she had been the real sustaining force behind his work. The tone of *When We Dead Awaken* is accordingly elegiac, an appropriate coda to Ibsen's long career. Two months later, in March 1900, he suffered the first of a series of strokes which was to lead to his death, in Kristiania, on 23 May 1906.

An Enemy of the People: What Happens in the Play

Acts One and Two take place in the living room of Dr Tomas Stockmann, medical superintendent of the municipal Baths in a small town in southern Norway. Stockmann's wife Katrine is serving supper to Billing, a journalist on the local newspaper, *The People's Courier*, while they wait for her husband and Billing's editor Hovstad to arrive. An unexpected caller, however, is Stockmann's brother Peter, the town's Mayor, joined soon after by Hovstad. The conversation becomes rather strained, owing to the Mayor's disapproval of the radical politics espoused by Hovstad's paper. And although they all agree on the outstanding benefits the Baths will bring to the town's flourishing economy, Hovstad's assertion that the credit belongs to the superintendent alone irritates the Mayor, and an argument is only averted by the arrival of Stockmann himself, accompanied by his two young sons, and an old family friend, Captain Horster.

Stockmann is in high spirits and proudly contrasts his new-found prosperity, thanks to his position as Baths superintendent, with the hardships of his former life as a poorly rewarded physician in the remote north of the country. Hovstad has called to collect an article Stockmann had promised to write about the Baths, but the doctor enigmatically hints at some new development, and his reluctance to explain further prompts the Mayor to accuse him of egotism, before indignantly leaving the house. After the Mayor's departure, Stockmann asks if that day's post has been delivered, while his guests discuss the forthcoming municipal elections. Hovstad and Billing rebuke Captain Horster for his freely confessed lack of interest in politics. Stockmann's daughter Petra, a schoolteacher, then arrives home bearing a letter for her father, which he immediately takes into his study to open, emerging triumphant a few moments later – the letter contains an analyst's report that a water sample from the Baths is seriously polluted. Stockmann's long-held opinion, rejected by the planning committee, that the water-supply system had been incorrectly installed, has now been vindicated. The Baths must be shut down for the entire system to be relaid, and Stockmann will instruct the board of directors to that effect. Hovstad asks permission to run the story in the *Courier*, and Act One ends in a spirit of joyful celebration.

At the beginning of Act Two, Stockmann is awaiting the arrival of the Mayor, who has now received the news of the analyst's report. However, it is his wife's foster-father, Morten Kiil, who first appears, and although sceptical of the existence of Stockmann's 'invisible' bacteria, he expresses delight at the embarrassment the story of the polluted Baths will cause the Mayor and council, against whom he has a long-standing grudge. Hovstad is next to arrive, and while Stockmann is initially startled by the editor's assertion that the Baths affair is symbolic of the essential rottenness at the core of the town's political establishment, he accepts the premise, regardless of the consequences, in the defence of truth. The pair are then joined by Aslaksen, the printer of *The People's Courier*, who in turn promises the support of the town's small-business community, while at the same time, rather to Hovstad's distaste, urging the necessity for moderation. As his guests leave, Stockmann asks Hovstad not to publish the damaging article about the Baths before the Mayor has had a chance to respond; if, however, the Mayor should refuse to act on Stockmann's advice, Hovstad and the *Courier* will take up the fight.

Buoyed up by these offers of support, Stockmann is able to confront the Mayor from a position of strength, and when the latter suggests a compromise, to avoid the loss of revenue attendant on closing the Baths, Stockmann accuses his brother of attempting to conceal his own part in the original flawed decision to install the inferior system which has caused the problem. The Mayor is insistent – the board of directors will keep the Baths open, until some long-term solution is found, and Stockmann must remain silent on the content of the analyst's report. Stockmann tells him that the whole matter is about to become public knowledge, through the pages of *The People's Courier*. The Mayor then warns him of potentially dire consequences for his family, and declares that Stockmann must publicly confess to having made a grave mistake and affirm his complete faith in the board of directors. However, if Stockmann persists in his misguided commitment to the truth at all costs, he is almost certain to lose his position at the Baths, and his respect in the community. His ultimatum delivered, the Mayor leaves, and Katrine and Petra, eavesdropping in the adjoining room, rush in. The idealistic and headstrong Petra urges her father to action, but Katrine, anxious for the future of their family, advises caution. In a show of defiance, Stockmann storms out, now even more determined to assert his rights as a free man.

Act Three takes place in the editorial office of *The People's Courier*, where Hovstad and Billing are preparing to publish Stockmann's article. They take special satisfaction from the fact that the Mayor's reputation will be damaged no matter how he handles the affair – if he endorses Stockmann's view, he risks incurring the wrath of the town's wealthy establishment; if he opposes the doctor, he will lose the support of the small businessmen and ratepayers, represented by the printer Aslaksen. With municipal elections imminent, this is very good news for the radical opposition, and the arrival of Stockmann, promising further incendiary articles on a daily basis, is seen as a godsend. Aslaksen, as ever, pleads for moderation, but Billing and Hovstad brush his objections aside. Later, Petra calls at the editorial office to return an English story which Hovstad had asked her to translate, and which she regards as unworthy of the *Courier* on the grounds of its falsity and sentimentality. Hovstad explains that Billing had intended it as a sort of 'sweetener' to make the more radical material seem acceptable. In an unguarded moment, Hovstad goes on to confess that his dedication to her father's cause is partly motivated by the attraction he feels for Petra. She takes exception to this and curtly dismisses him.

After Petra leaves, the Mayor comes in search of Stockmann's article. In the course of conversation, he manages to convince

Aslaksen and Hovstad that the drastic measures being insisted
upon by his brother will seriously damage the town's economy,
with the burden of increased taxation to pay for them falling
most heavily on those who can least afford it, including the
small-business community represented by Aslaksen. The
Mayor then suggests that the *Courier* should suppress
Stockmann's controversial article and replace it with one
written by himself, proposing a long-term compromise
solution. At this point, Stockmann is seen approaching the
office, and the Mayor hurriedly withdraws to an adjoining
room. Stockmann is not unduly perturbed to find that his
article is not yet ready to proofread, and modestly insists that
there should be no great display of public gratitude when it
does appear. An embarrassed Hovstad is about to disabuse
him, when the doctor's wife arrives, urging her husband to
consider the implications for his family if the article is printed.
Stockmann, confident of the support of the 'solid majority',
dismisses Katrine's fears and, even when he flushes his
shamefaced brother out of his hiding place, continues to
maintain his triumphant stance. Aslaksen and Hovstad are
then forced to confess that they can no longer publish his
article in the *Courier*. Stockmann, defiant to the end, declares
he will proclaim the truth from every street corner, and
Katrine vows to stand by him.

Act Four takes place in a large room in Captain Horster's
house, where Dr Stockmann and the other interested parties
are to address a public meeting. It is Stockmann's intention to
denounce the Mayor, but before he can begin, Aslaksen moves
that a chairman be elected, and the Mayor proposes Aslaksen
himself. The latter duly takes the chair, urging moderation, his
constant watchword, and the Mayor swiftly acts to gag his
brother, forbidding Stockmann to make any reference to the
alleged pollution of the water supply. He then advocates his

own plan to deal with the problem, and warns of the ruinous costs of the doctor's radical alternative. Aslaksen suggests that Stockmann's real motive is to disrupt the ordered society of the town, and Hovstad follows his lead, claiming that the doctor appears to have no support even from readers of the *Courier*. Stockmann promises to make no mention of the Baths, but when he is finally allowed to speak, he launches an attack on the town's ruling elite, in particular his own brother, accusing them of polluting the very lives of their fellow-citizens through routine double-dealing and corruption. As a consequence, the entire community is based on a fundamental lie, upheld by that same solid majority, who are the greatest enemies of society, more so even than their political masters.

Stockmann's speech ends in uproar, and, when the meeting is eventually called to order, Aslaksen asks him to withdraw his comments. Stockmann not only refuses but goes on to challenge the basic premise of democracy, arguing that it cannot be justified, since the majority of the people are ignorant and stupid, unfitted to hold sway over the enlightened minority, who are by definition always right. His audience is further outraged when he develops his argument by citing the example of pure-bred animals, superior in every way to hybrids, and compares the majority of people to mongrels. These, he says, are regarded by Hovstad and his like as the bedrock of society. True breadth of mind, on the other hand, is morality in action, and possessed only by those of rare spiritual and intellectual gifts. Rather than see his hometown flourish on a foundation of lies, Stockmann announces his intention to destroy it by speaking the truth at every opportunity. In response, Hovstad calls upon the meeting to proclaim Dr Stockmann an enemy of the people, and a resolution is passed to that effect. Meanwhile, Morten Kiil asks Stockmann if he also intends to identify his tannery as the source of the pollution to the Baths water supply, and warns him of unnamed dire consequences. The meeting then concludes in acrimonious exchanges, and the Stockmann family leave to go home, cries of 'Enemy of the people!' ringing in their ears.

Act Five is set in the doctor's study, the floor strewn with stones and broken window-glass. Katrine brings Tomas a letter; it is in fact an eviction notice, and she is soon followed by Petra, who has been dismissed from her teaching position. Captain Horster, who had generously offered Stockmann his room for the ill-fated meeting, is next to arrive, likewise dismissed from his post. The bad news is then compounded by the arrival of the Mayor, to inform Stockmann that not only is he to lose his position as medical superintendent of the Baths, but also most of his patients in the town. However, should Stockmann be willing to wait until the furore has died down, then apologise, and withdraw his claims of pollution, the Mayor is confident he will be accepted back into the community. Stockmann vehemently rejects the idea, and the Mayor accuses him of maintaining his defiant stance on expectations from old Morten Kiil's will; Kiil is a long-standing political enemy of the Mayor, and indeed to the Mayor's way of thinking, Stockmann's every action from the outset has been at the behest of Morten Kiil.

As the Mayor leaves, Morten Kiil himself arrives. Conscience-stricken by the realisation that his tannery has been poisoning the town's water supply, he has taken the extraordinary step of using the money he had set aside for Katrine's inheritance to purchase as many shares as he could afford in the polluted municipal Baths. Stockmann now faces a terrible dilemma – if he goes ahead with his plan to publicise the state of the Baths, he will render Katrine's inheritance worthless. Moreover, Kiil must have an answer by two o'clock. No sooner has Kiil departed, however, than Hovstad and Aslaksen apppear. They are convinced that Stockmann had exaggerated the whole pollution affair in order to enable Morten Kiil to buy up the shares, and they offer to put *The People's Courier* at his disposal to continue his campaign, further assuring him of the support of Aslaksen's small-business community – all on condition that he finance the paper. If he refuses, however, they will use their influence to destroy him. Stockmann drives them from his house in a towering rage. He then sends Petra to deliver an emphatic 'no' in answer to her grandfather's ultimatum. He is more determined than ever to stay and fight. Captain Horster offers them board and lodging so they can remain in town, and their two boys will be withdrawn from school and educated at home. The Stockmann family, united in adversity, now prepare to meet a hostile world head-on, and, as the curtain falls, Stockmann, overjoyed, has made a new discovery: the strongest man in the world is the one who stands most alone.

The Whistleblower as Hero

Ibsen's Dr Tomas Stockmann is sourced in the first instance from two real-life 'heroes': one, a Dr Meissner in the 1830s, a practitioner in the Bohemian spa resort of Teplitz, who made public an outbreak of cholera at the height of the tourist season, prompting the enraged citizens to storm his house and drive him from the town; the other, a chemist, Harald Thaulow, who led a lengthy campaign against the unsanitary conditions of the Kristiania Steam Kitchens, culminating in his being prevented from delivering a public speech on the matter in February 1881, in circumstances very similar to those experienced by Stockmann: the event was reported in detail in the Kristiania daily *Aftonposten*. The touchpaper, however, which would ignite the raw materials of *An Enemy of the People*, begun in the spring of 1882, was Ibsen's fury at the treatment *Ghosts* had received, in particular from the so-called liberal press, on its publication a few months earlier.

The theme of the heroic individual voice against the abuse of power, in whatever form – State tyranny, commercial or industrial exploitation, vested interests of all shapes and sizes – has a history reaching back to antiquity, most memorably to Socrates' defiance of the Athenian establishment, forward to our own day, when scarcely a week passes without fresh examples making the headlines. The scale has of course expanded beyond imagining: the phenomenon of WikiLeaks, set in motion by Julian Assange, now enables a lowly United States Army private to press a computer key and instantly flood the world with vast amounts of data exposing military skulduggery in Iraq and Afghanistan. And while the whistleblower hero's motives may not always be untainted, the classic response of those exposed is not to mend their ways but to shoot the messenger, or make him drink hemlock, as custom demands.

It is no surprise, given the nature of the world we live in, that tales of the lone individual doing battle against gigantic corporations, secretive and soulless bureaucracies, ruthless exploiters of our every human weakness, not least the unreasoning blind faith we place in them, should rank high amongst our most enduring myths. The cinema is especially rich in the whistleblowing genre: memorable examples include *The China Syndrome* (1979) and *Silkwood* (1983), concerning safety violations in the nuclear industry; *The Insider* (1999) and *The Informant* (2009), targeting the tobacco companies and agri-business; two different films titled *The Whistleblower* (1987 and 2010), on the subject of paranoid secrecy in the military and intelligence communities; *Enron: The Smartest Guys in the Room* (2005), documenting massive fraud in the world of high finance; *Erin Brockovich* (2000), which revisits Ibsen's theme of toxic waste leaking into a town's water supply, compounded by crooked insurance practices. A more direct link with Ibsen, finally, may be seen in the 1975 thriller *Jaws*, based on Peter Benchley's novel, in which the waterborne threat is a great white shark, terrorising the Atlantic beach-resort town of Amity. Like his counterpart in *An Enemy of the People*, Amity's Mayor is determined to play down the threat, fearing the loss of revenue at the highpoint of the tourist season. Interestingly, though, the whistleblowing role is shared among three characters: the town's elected, and therefore vulnerable, police chief; a bookish ichthyologist; and a professional hunter, a sort of alcoholic Captain Ahab of the shark world. Arguably, the character of the police chief is insufficiently complex to sustain interest as a lone hero, and in that respect it is instructive to turn to Arthur Miller's 1950 adaptation of *An Enemy of the People*, which presents us with a Dr Stockmann also less complex than Ibsen's original.

Miller's version, which incidentally transferred to the cinema in a somewhat underrated 1978 film starring the late Steve McQueen, is reputed to be more often revived in the United States than Ibsen's, and it is undoubtedly less challenging, largely due to its treatment of the central character. For a start, Miller reduces Ibsen's five acts to three, and it is perhaps ironic that, writing during the heyday of McCarthyism and rampant anti-Communist paranoia, his most noteworthy excisions amount to a 'cleaning up' of the hero's politics, suppressing Stockmann's now unfashionable views on eugenics – itself an act of literary censorship. Miller removes all reference to the selective breeding of hens and dogs as a blueprint for human development, and inserts a parable of a pathfinder, who returns to alert his comrades to an enemy ambush on the road ahead, but whose warning goes disastrously unheeded. At the finale of Miller's adaptation, Stockmann also expands his outlook to include his family: 'But remember now, everybody… we're the strongest people in the world…'

But the anti-democratic views of Ibsen's original Stockmann are not so easily sidestepped, and there is abundant evidence, in Ibsen's correspondence with the Danish critic Georg Brandes and others, that he endorsed to the hilt Stockmann's jaundiced views on majority rule, though it must be said that the doctor's disenchantment comes upon him only after he is betrayed, in the crucial Act Three confrontation with the Mayor in the *Courier* office; earlier, he had positively rejoiced at Aslaksen's offer to deliver his meekly biddable homeowners and tea-drinkers – his 'solid majority' – to his cause. From then on, however, Stockmann is virtually overwhelmed by a rising tide of vested interests and left powerless, save for the strength of his convictions. *An Enemy of the People* plainly solicits its audience's vote for Stockmann, at the same time as it questions their competence. In 1905, at the time of the abortive first Russian revolution, the Moscow Art Theatre production in St Petersburg was cheered to the echo, and Stanislavsky, who played Stockmann, was mobbed by ecstatic workers, rushing onstage to shake his hand, evidently willing to overlook his character's more contentious opinions.

An Enemy of the People presents us with an open-and-shut case. Stockmann *is* in the right, and apart from Morten Kiil, who hasn't quite caught up with Pasteur, no one disputes the doctor's assertion that the Baths are polluted. Neither Peter Stockmann nor anyone else suggests trawling for a more anodyne second opinion, and the issue centres rather on what use each character makes of the toxic information. The Mayor's first move, in line with his civic duty, at least as he sees it, is to obtain a cost estimate of his brother's radical solution. Unsurprisingly, he chooses to kick the problem into the long grass, calculating that a few more sick tourists in the warm weather will be less damaging than the possible collapse of the burgeoning local economy. In a word, he reacts like the shrewd political animal he undoubtedly is, and men of his sort take no prisoners.

Among the forces eventually ranged against the doctor, Billing and Aslaksen can be readily enough dismissed. Billing is an uncouth hypocrite, secretly touting for a job on the council payroll at the same time as he calls for red revolution. Aslaksen is a prissy old bore, a committee man to his fingertips, obsessed with sederunts and quorums, and fundamentally stupid. The wonder is that Stockmann doesn't spot this the second Aslaksen opens his mouth – certainly the audience does. That leaves Hovstad, the brains of the operation, and it is interesting to learn that Ibsen, prior to the first performance of *An Enemy of the People* at the Kristiania Theatre, wrote to the director Hans Schroeder offering a thumbnail sketch of Hovstad's character, in which he emphasised the extreme deprivation of the latter's childhood, in terms reminiscent of the life he ascribes to the ill-bred mongrels of his extended comparison in Act Four. Hovstad's physical attributes and demeanour, Ibsen suggests, should reflect his poverty-stricken upbringing, and goes on to observe that the lower orders seldom possess the appearance of heroes.

Ibsen, both in *An Enemy of the People* and in his correspondence, persistently attacks the modern sacred cow of democracy, and the party system by which it is routinely enacted. His view, that it merely replaces absolute monarchy, say, with an equally oppressive tyranny of the witless majority, is given weight in Hovstad's driving ambition, to unseat the town's incumbent rulers and install his own 'radical' party – exchanging one grasping hand on the levers of power for another. We cannot assume that Hovstad is blind to the real dangers posed by the polluted water supply, but the political advantage Stockmann's discovery offers is a golden opportunity. Nor can we assume that his interest in Petra is entirely motivated by the desire to profit from Morten Kiil's legacy, though that too would be a bonus. However, Petra herself knows nothing of her grandfather's intentions when she abruptly sends Hovstad packing, and on the face of it, she seems remarkably thin-skinned, a trait perhaps inherited from her father, whose tolerance of human frailty is similarly limited.

Stockmann, as Ibsen himself avers in his correspondence, frequently acts as his creator's spokesman, and we are entitled to take his opinions on the ideal form of government seriously; decision-making, in Ibsen's view, should be left to an elite, self-appointed, presumably – some kind of intellectual or spiritual aristocracy. In Stockmann's reflection on mongrels and poodles, however, the superiority of the latter, well-fed, comfortably housed, exposed from birth to high culture and *politesse*, appears to be acquired by accident of birth, and might stand comparison with the largely Eton and Oxbridge-trained elite whose dominance, at the time of writing, makes the United Kingdom arguably the least representative democracy in the developed world.

Unless we take Stockmann at his own valuation, it is difficult for a modern audience to engage uncritically with him as the hero, bloody but unbowed, who brings down the curtain as 'the strongest man in the world', standing alone, albeit flanked by Katrine, Petra, Morten, Eilif, and the loyal Captain Horster. Randine, the slatternly maid whose name he can never remember, has doubtless left to seek alternative employment. For the future, meanwhile, Stockmann will rescue twelve 'mongrels' from the mean streets to become his disciples, for the work of building his version of Plato's ideal republic. Stockmann is of course unjustly persecuted by a coalition of the corrupt and self-serving, none of whom is fit to tie his shoe-laces, but there is more than a hint of megalomania in his make-up.

The debate Stockmann initiates on heredity and upbringing, in relation to character, entitles us to speculate on his own. His alleged descent from 'some old Pomeranian pirate' is a romantic whimsy, however, and his more recent past, the years spent in self-imposed exile, living from hand to mouth in a frozen northern wilderness, is of far more interest. Ibsen offers no explanation for this life choice, and Stockmann's scathing comment on the inhabitants being more in need of a vet than a physician hardly suggests a self-sacrificing mission. A likelier explanation, perhaps, with a bearing on Stockmann's long-standing feud with his brother Peter, is that he was simply unable to obtain a more rewarding urban practice. And while the initial idea for the Baths was his, its implementation, the raising of investment capital for their construction, and so forth, would assuredly have been beyond his competence. The fact that the investors then chose to maximise their profits by compromising on safety is a regrettable, but entirely predictable outcome. Stockmann, however, is resentful not only at being kept out of the loop, but also of the fact that his one genuinely successful venture in life is being hijacked by his brother. Consequently, his reaction to the analyst's damning report on the water supply is not alarm, but triumph. And if one were in any doubt as to the doctor's more questionable motives, his comical pantomime in the *Courier* office, strutting up and down with the Mayor's cap and cane, confirms that his commitment to the truth is tainted by sibling rivalry. One may wonder also whether the doctor's young sons, given the choice as the free and independent young men he plans to make of them, might not rather have inherited Morten Kiil's fortune than their father's absurd memorial cairn.

Finally, none of this makes Ibsen's Stockmann any less of a hero in the honourable tradition of the whistleblower, even though much of what he says and does may cause the dispassionate observer to cringe, or to echo Voltaire: *J'aime pas les héros – ils font trop de bruit* ('I don't like heroes, they make too much noise'). In the theatre, however, it is the flaws in Stockmann's character which make him convincingly human, complex and fascinating. And perhaps significantly, Ibsen gives the last word, the final verdict of *An Enemy of the People*, not to his self-proclaimed strongest man, but to be shared between his exasperated, infinitely patient wife, and his enraptured daughter: *Oh, Tomas!… Father!*

An Enemy of the People on Stage

Generally speaking, Ibsen regulated his dramatic output in a thoroughly professional manner, publishing a new play every two years, timed to catch the peak sales period at Christmas, and ahead of production. *An Enemy of the People* is exceptional in that it was published in November 1882, while the critical furore aroused by *Ghosts*, published the previous winter, was still in the forefront of his mind. There is also evidence that Ibsen had been planning the play much earlier, and most likely completed it well ahead of his self-imposed schedule, in mid-June 1882.

An Enemy of the People, one of Ibsen's longest mature plays, and a savage critique of Norwegian provincial attitudes and values, nonetheless achieved a decent run of twenty-seven performances following its Kristiania premiere in January 1883, before being staged in the other Scandinavian capitals. Ibsen's instructions to the director of the Kristiania Theatre, incidentally, were particularly insistent on absolute naturalism in every aspect of the production. In May 1888, Duke Georg II of Saxe-Meiningen, whose revolutionary approach to set design and performance had been a major influence on Ibsen's first 'realist' play, *Pillars of the Community* (1877), directed *An Enemy of the People* in a German translation at the Hoftheater. Its English premiere took place at the Haymarket on 14 June 1893, with Herbert Beerbohm Tree as Dr Stockmann. And although the play had been presented at Korsh's private theatre in Moscow as early as 1891, the Moscow Art Theatre first staged it in October 1900, with Konstantin Stanislavsky as Stockmann, a role he reprised in St Petersburg in 1905, when its powerful rhetoric caused a near-riot in the tense atmosphere of the abortive first Russian revolution. *An Enemy of the People* was incidentally the first Ibsen play to be performed by the Comédie Française, though not until 1921.

An Enemy of the People is much less often staged than Ibsen's other great realist plays. One reason might be that, unless a decent-sized crowd can be mustered for Act Four, it tends to fall rather flat. Apart from the stringent economics of the professional theatre, attitudes to the views expressed in the play have changed radically over the past century. Arthur Miller's adaptation may have breathed new life into it, but following its premiere on 28 December 1950 at the Broadhurst Theatre, New York, with Fredric March as Stockmann, it enjoyed only modest success. However,

An Enemy of the People made a notable UK appearance at the Chichester Festival in 1975, starring Donald Sinden, and curiously, the BBC broadcast a television adaptation of the play in 1980, transferred to a Scottish setting in which Robert Urquhart became 'Tom Stockman'. Then in late 1988, Arthur Miller's adaptation, directed by David Thacker, was successfully revived at the Young Vic, where it won high praise, in particular for Tom Wilkinson's performance as Stockmann. In more recent times, the National Theatre production of Christopher Hampton's version, directed by Trevor Nunn and premiered in September 1997, with Ian McKellen as Stockmann and Stephen Moore as the Mayor, was widely acclaimed both in the UK and the United States. Finally, the newly refurbished Crucible Theatre in Sheffield opened its production of *An Enemy of the People* in February 2010, directed by Daniel Evans, and featuring an outstanding energetic performance by Antony Sher as Stockmann, ably supported by John Shrapnel's Mayor.

Ibsen: Key Dates

1828   Born 20 March in Skien, south-east Norway

1835   Father's business fails, family moves to Venstøp

1844   Ibsen leaves school, becomes apprentice pharmacist
        in Grimstad

1846   Aged eighteen, Ibsen fathers illegitimate son by
        housemaid Else Sofie Jensdatter

1849   First play, *Catiline*, rejected by Kristiania Danish
        Theatre

1850   Fails university entrance exam. Premiere of *The
        Warrior's Barrow*, 26 September, Kristiania Theatre

1851   Appointed writer-in-residence at Bergen Norwegian
        Theatre, to write a play each year for five years

1853   *St John's Night*

1854   *The Warrior's Barrow* revised

1855   *Lady Inger of Østråt*

1856   *The Feast at Solhaug*

1857   Final contracted play for Bergen Theatre, *Olaf
        Liljekrans*. Appointed artistic director at Norwegian
        Theatre in Kristiania

1858   Marries Suzannah Thoresen, 18 June. *The Vikings at
        Helgeland*

For Further Reading

The Norwegian text of *An Enemy of the People* (*En folkefiende*) is published by Gyldendal Norsk Forlag, Oslo, 1978. James McFarlane's translation, published in Volume VI of the Oxford *Ibsen*, Oxford University Press, 1977, includes a useful commentary on the play, while the same author's *Cambridge Companion to Ibsen*, Cambridge University Press, 1994, brings together essays by a number of distinguished critics. George B. Bryan's *An Ibsen Companion*, Greenwood Press, Westport, Conn., 1984, is an invaluable guide, in dictionary format, to Ibsen's life and work. A handy quick reference function is also served by *A Pocket Guide to Ibsen, Chekhov and Strindberg*, by Michael Pennington and Stephen Unwin, Faber and Faber, 2004. Michael Meyer's three-volume *Henrik Ibsen*, revised in 1992, and available in a condensed version, published by Penguin Books, 1985, is justly regarded as the authoritative work on Ibsen's life, and the theatre and politics of his day.

Early reviews of all Ibsen's plays are collected in *Ibsen: The Critical Heritage*, ed. Michael Egan, Routledge and Kegan Paul, 1972, while the pioneering endeavours of William Archer in bringing Ibsen to the attention of the English-speaking world are commemorated in *William Archer on Ibsen: The Major Essays 1889–1919*, ed. Thomas Postlewait, Greenwood Press, Westport, Conn., 1984. George Bernard Shaw's 1891 essay, *The Quintessence of Ibsenism*, Hill & Wang, New York, 1957, is also of historical importance. More recent scholarship includes John Northam's *Ibsen: A Critical Study*, Cambridge University Press, 1973, and Ronald Gray's stimulating *Ibsen:*

A Dissenting View, Cambridge University Press, 1977. Richard Hornby's *Patterns in Ibsen's Middle Plays*, Associated University Presses, 1981, and Brian Johnston's *Text and Supertext in Ibsen's Drama*, Pennsylvania State University Press, 1989, are also valuable studies. Finally, Robert Ferguson's *Henrik Ibsen – A New Biography*, Richard Cohen Books, 1996, is a fascinating portrayal of a deeply troubled spirit.

AN ENEMY OF THE PEOPLE

Characters

DR TOMAS STOCKMANN, *medical officer at the municipal Baths*

MRS KATRINE STOCKMANN, *his wife*

PETRA, *their daughter, a teacher*

EILIF *and* MORTEN, *their sons, aged thirteen and ten respectively*

MAYOR PETER STOCKMANN, *the doctor's elder brother, Mayor, police chief, chairman of the Baths Committee, etc.*

MORTEN KIIL, *a tanner, Mrs Stockmann's adoptive father*

HOVSTAD, *editor of* The People's Courier *newspaper*

BILLING, *his assistant*

CAPTAIN HORSTER

ASLAKSEN, *a printer*

People at a public meeting – men of various social classes, a few women, and a crowd of schoolboys.

The action takes place in a coastal town in southern Norway.

ACT ONE

It is evening. DR STOCKMANN's *living room, simply but comfortably furnished. Two doors at right, the farther leading to the entrance hall, the nearer to the doctor's study. At left, directly opposite the hall door, is a door leading to the family's living quarters. In the middle of the same wall stands the stove, downstage of which is a settee with a mirror hanging above it, and an oval table, covered with a cloth, in front of it. There is a lamp on the table, shaded and lit. Upstage, in the back wall, is an open door leading to the dining room, where a table set for dinner, with a lit lamp on it, can be seen.* BILLING, *his napkin tucked under his chin, is sitting at the dinner table, while* MRS STOCKMANN, *standing nearby, is passing him a large plate of roast beef. The other places at the table are empty, and the settings in some disorder, showing that a meal has recently been eaten.*

MRS STOCKMANN. Well, if you will come an hour late, Mr Billing, you must expect cold food.

BILLING (*eating*). This is excellent – absolutely perfect.

MRS STOCKMANN. You know how particular my husband is about regular mealtimes.

BILLING. I don't mind in the least. Actually, I think food tastes better like this, when I can eat alone, in peace and quiet.

MRS STOCKMANN. Yes, well – as long as you're enjoying it. (*Turns towards the hall door, listening.*) That must be Hovstad…

BILLING. Very likely.

The MAYOR, *Peter Stockmann, enters, wearing an overcoat and his official cap, and carrying a walking stick.*

MAYOR. A very good evening to you, Katrine.

MRS STOCKMANN (*coming into the living room*). Why, it's you – good evening! How nice of you to stop by and see us.

MAYOR. Well, I happened to be passing, so… (*Glances towards the dining room.*) Ah, I see you have company.

MRS STOCKMANN (*a little embarrassed*). No, no – he's just dropped in, we weren't expecting anybody. (*Hurriedly.*) Why don't you join him, and have a bite to eat?

MAYOR. Who, me? No, thank you. Good heavens, a cooked meal at night? Not with *my* digestion.

MRS STOCKMANN. Oh, just this once, surely…

MAYOR. No, honestly, it's very kind of you, but I'll stick to my tea and toast – it's healthier in the long run, and a bit more economical too.

MRS STOCKMANN (*smiles*). Now, you mustn't run away with the idea that Tomas and I are terrible spendthrifts.

MAYOR. Not *you*, dear Katrine – nothing could be further from my mind. (*Points to the* DOCTOR's *study.*) So he isn't at home?

MRS STOCKMANN. No, he's just gone out for an after-dinner stroll – and the boys are with him.

MAYOR. Hm, does that really do any good, I wonder? (*Listens.*) That'll be him now.

MRS STOCKMANN. No, I don't think so.

A knock at the door.

Come in!

HOVSTAD *enters from the hallway.*

Oh, it's you, Mr Hovstad…

HOVSTAD. Yes, I'm sorry, you'll have to excuse me, but I got held up at the printing shop. Good evening, Mr Mayor.

MAYOR *(bowing a little stiffly).* Mr Hovstad. A business call, no doubt?

HOVSTAD. In part, yes. It's about something that's to go into the paper.

MAYOR. I thought as much. I hear my brother's become an extremely prolific contributor to *The People's Courier.*

HOVSTAD. Yes, whenever he has a few home truths to tell, he does a piece for the *Courier.*

MRS STOCKMANN *(to* HOVSTAD). Are you sure you wouldn't like to… *(Gesturing towards the dining room.)*

MAYOR. Well, good heavens, I'm not blaming him. After all, he's simply addressing himself to the sort of reader most likely to be sympathetic to his views. Anyway, speaking personally, I've no reason to harbour any ill feeling towards your paper, Mr Hovstad.

HOVSTAD. No, I should hope not.

MAYOR. Taken by and large, there's an admirable spirit of tolerance in this town of ours – genuine public-spiritedness. And that derives from the fact that we have a great civic enterprise to unite us – an enterprise which concerns every right-minded citizen in equal measure…

HOVSTAD. The Baths, yes.

MAYOR. Precisely. We have our splendid new municipal Baths. Mark my words, Mr Hovstad, those Baths are set to become the town's very lifeblood. Without a doubt, sir.

MRS STOCKMANN. Yes, Tomas says that too…

MAYOR. You know, it's quite extraordinary how things have improved this past year or two. People have money to spend, there's more life, more of a buzz about the town. Land and property values are going up day by day.

HOVSTAD. And unemployment's going down.

MAYOR. Yes, that's true. The burden of public assistance has been lessened too, much to the relief of property-owners, and that's likely to be reduced still further, if we have a decent summer this year – plenty of visitors, lots of invalids, to spread the word about our famous Baths.

HOVSTAD. And things are looking very promising in that regard, so I'm told.

MAYOR. All the signs are favourable. We're getting more and more enquiries about accommodation and suchlike every day.

HOVSTAD. Well, then, the doctor's article will be very much to the point.

MAYOR. He's written another piece?

HOVSTAD. Well, it's something he wrote in winter, recommending the Baths, and giving an account of the superb health-giving qualities of the life here. But I held the article over at the time.

MAYOR. Ah, there'd be one or two flaws in it, I suppose?

HOVSTAD. No, not at all. I just thought it was better to wait until the spring. This is when people start thinking about their summer holidays.

MAYOR. That's right. That makes good sense, Mr Hovstad.

MRS STOCKMANN. Yes, Tomas will stick at nothing when it has to do with the Baths.

MAYOR. Well, he *is* one of the office-bearers.

HOVSTAD. Yes, indeed – in fact, it was the doctor who first came up with the idea.

MAYOR. Really? You think so? Yes, I've heard quite a few folk express that opinion. But I rather fancied I played a modest part in that undertaking myself.

MRS STOCKMANN. Yes, that's what Tomas always says.

HOVSTAD. Well, of course, Mr Mayor – no one would deny it. You set the whole business going as a practical concern, everybody knows that. All I meant was that the initial idea for the Baths came from the doctor.

MAYOR. Yes, my brother's never been short of ideas in his time – more's the pity. But when there's real work to be done, you need a different sort of man, Mr Hovstad. And to be quite frank, I would've thought that in this house, at the very least…

MRS STOCKMANN. Peter, dear – please…

HOVSTAD. Mr Mayor, how could you imagine…

MRS STOCKMANN. Go and get yourself something to eat, Mr Hovstad, while you're waiting – I'm sure my husband won't be long.

HOVSTAD. Well, thanks – perhaps just a bite. (*Goes into the dining room.*)

MAYOR (*in an undertone*). It's funny, but these people from peasant stock never seem to have any tact.

MRS STOCKMANN. You're not letting that bother you, surely? Can't you and Tomas simply share the credit, like brothers?

MAYOR. Well, I daresay we should. But not everybody, it seems, is content to share.

MRS STOCKMANN. Oh, that's nonsense. You and Tomas are in complete agreement on these things. (*Listens.*) I think that's him coming now. (*Goes to open the door leading into the hall.*)

DR STOCKMANN (*laughing and talking outside*). Here you are, Katrine, another visitor for you! Isn't this a treat? Come in, Captain Horster, please do – just hang your coat up there, on that peg. Oh, you're not wearing an overcoat, I see. Would you believe it, Katrine, I ran into him in the street, and had the devil of a job persuading him to come.

CAPTAIN HORSTER *enters, and greets* MRS STOCKMANN.

(*In the doorway.*) In you go, my lads. They're absolutely starving. Now, come along, Captain Horster – you must have a nice bit of roast beef…

He propels HORSTER *towards the dining room, and the boys,* EILIF *and* MORTEN, *follow him in.*

MRS STOCKMANN. But, Tomas – don't you see…?

DR STOCKMANN (*turning in the doorway*). Oh, it's you, Peter! (*Goes over to shake his hand.*) Well, now, this is a *real* treat.

MAYOR. Unfortunately, I have to be going in a minute…

DR STOCKMANN. Oh, nonsense! There's some hot toddy coming up soon. Katrine, you haven't forgotten the toddy, have you?

MRS STOCKMANN. Indeed, no. The water's already boiling. (*Goes into the kitchen.*)

MAYOR. Toddy as well?

DR STOCKMANN. Yes, sit down, do, and we'll enjoy it in comfort.

MAYOR. Thanks, but I don't go in much for drinking sessions.

DR STOCKMANN. This isn't a drinking session.

MAYOR. Well, it looks to me as if… (*Glancing towards the dining room.*) It's astonishing how much food these people can put away.

DR STOCKMANN (*rubbing his hands*). Yes, isn't it wonderful to see young folk eating? They've got boundless appetites, and that's just how it should be. They need their food, to give them strength! They're the ones who'll be stirring things up in the years to come, Peter.

MAYOR. And exactly what, may I ask, needs 'stirring up' here, as you put it?

DR STOCKMANN. Oh, that's something you'll have to ask the younger generation, when the time comes. We can't see it, of course. I mean, that goes without saying – old fogeys like you and me.

MAYOR. Well, really! That's a most peculiar description…

DR STOCKMANN. Oh, you mustn't take me too literally, Peter. I'm just so full of the joys of living, you see, so very

happy and contented. I think we're extraordinarily lucky to
be alive at such a time, in the midst of all this germinating,
flourishing life. This truly is a wonderful age we live in! It's
as if a whole new world was being created all around us.

MAYOR. Is that honestly what you think?

DR STOCKMANN. Yes, I do – although of course you can't
see it as clearly as I do. You've spent your entire life here, in
the same environment, so your impressions have become
blunted. Whereas I was away all those years, stuck up in
the far north, almost never encountering a new face, let
alone any fresh ideas. For me now it's as if I've been
transported to the heart of some great teeming
metropolis…

MAYOR. Hah, metropolis, indeed!

DR STOCKMANN. Yes, well, I know everything's on a small
scale here compared with a lot of other places. But there's
life here, there's real promise, countless things to work and
strive for, and that's what matters… (*Pauses.*) Katrine, has
the postman been yet?

MRS STOCKMANN (*from the dining room*). No, not yet.

DR STOCKMANN. And having a decent salary too, Peter!
That's something you learn to appreciate, when you've
lived on the breadline, as we did.

MAYOR. Oh, good heavens…

DR STOCKMANN. No, truly – we had a pretty hard life up
there at times. And now I live like a gentleman. For
example, we had roast beef for lunch today. Yes, indeed,
and we had it again for supper. Are you sure you won't
have a little taste? At least let me show you what there is.
Come here…

MAYOR. No, no, there's no need, please.

DR STOCKMANN. Come here, anyway – we have a new tablecloth, have you seen it?

MAYOR. Yes, I did notice.

DR STOCKMANN. And a lampshade, d'you see? All out of what Katrine's managed to save. It makes the room really cosy now, don't you think? Just stand here for a moment – no, no, not there – look, wait, I'll show you. Now, see – the way it lights up the place – I think it's really elegant, don't you?

MAYOR. Oh, well – if you can afford these sort of luxuries…

DR STOCKMANN. These days I can. Katrine says I'm earning almost as much as we spend!

MAYOR. Almost as much, yes.

DR STOCKMANN. Well, a man of science ought to have a decent lifestyle. I'm sure any number of civil servants spend more in a year than I do.

MAYOR. I can well believe it – a top civil servant, a senior magistrate…

DR STOCKMANN. Well, let's say a simple businessman. Someone like that spends a lot more…

MAYOR. That depends on the circumstances.

DR STOCKMANN. Anyway, I don't squander my money on any old thing, Peter. But I do feel I can't deny myself the pleasure of entertaining people. It's something I need, you see, having spent so long cut off from things. It's an essential part of life for me, I've got to have the company of young folk, eager, outspoken, liberal-minded, energetic

– the sort of people you'll see here eating so heartily at my table. I just wish you knew Hovstad a little better…

MAYOR. Yes, as a matter of fact, Hovstad was telling me he's going to print another one of your articles.

DR STOCKMANN. Another of my articles?

MAYOR. Yes, about the Baths. Something you wrote last winter.

DR STOCKMANN. Oh, yes, that! No, I don't want that to go in right now.

MAYOR. No? I'd have thought this was the ideal time.

DR STOCKMANN. Well, yes – under ordinary circumstances, I suppose… (*Begins pacing the room.*)

MAYOR (*observing him*). So what's extraordinary about circumstances now?

DR STOCKMANN (*stops pacing*). I'm sorry, Peter, but I honestly can't tell you – not this evening, at any rate. There could be something quite extraordinary about the circumstances, or it could be nothing at all. In fact, it could well be just my imagination.

MAYOR. I must confess, it all sounds very mysterious. Is something wrong? Is there something you're keeping from me? I would remind you that as chairman of the Baths Committee…

DR STOCKMANN. And I would remind *you*… Oh, look, Peter, let's not fly off the handle at each other.

MAYOR. Heaven forbid! I'm not in the habit of flying off the handle, as you put it. But I must insist, most emphatically, that any steps deemed necessary should be taken through the proper channels, and carried out in a businesslike manner, by the legally constituted authorities. I can't allow any devious or underhand procedures.

DR STOCKMANN. Now, when have I ever been devious or underhand?

MAYOR. You have an inherent tendency to go your own way, all the same, and in a well-ordered society that's just as reprehensible. The individual must learn to subordinate his interests to those of the community at large – or more precisely, to those authorities charged with the common good.

DR STOCKMANN. That may well be, but what the devil has it got to do with me?

MAYOR. Because, my dear Tomas, it's something you apparently don't wish to accept. And if you're not careful, one of these days you'll pay dearly for it. So don't say I didn't warn you. Goodbye.

DR STOCKMANN. Have you taken leave of your senses? You're on completely the wrong track...

MAYOR. That would be most unlikely. Anyway, if I may be excused...? (*Calls into the dining room.*) Goodnight, Katrine! Goodnight, gentlemen! (*Goes out.*)

MRS STOCKMANN (*entering the living room*). Has he gone?

DR STOCKMANN. Indeed he has – and in high dudgeon.

MRS STOCKMANN. Oh, Tomas, what have you done to him this time?

DR STOCKMANN. Absolutely nothing. He simply can't expect me to give him accounts before they fall due.

MRS STOCKMANN. What does he want the accounts for?

DR STOCKMANN. Hm… Anyway, leave it to me, Katrine. You know, it's strange the postman hasn't come yet.

HOVSTAD, BILLING *and* HORSTER *have risen from the table and now come into the living room. They are shortly followed by* EILIF *and* MORTEN.

BILLING (*stretching his arms*). Ah, after a meal like that – I swear to God, you feel like a new man!

HOVSTAD. The Mayor wasn't in the best of humours this evening.

DR STOCKMANN. It's his stomach – he suffers from indigestion.

HOVSTAD. More likely it's us two from the *Courier* he can't stomach.

MRS STOCKMANN. Really? I thought you were getting on rather well with him.

HOVSTAD. Yes, it's a kind of armed truce, that's all.

BILLING. That's it exactly. There's no other word for it.

DR STOCKMANN. We must remember that Peter's a lonely man, poor chap. He has no real home, nowhere he can relax – it's business, business all the time. And that damned weak tea he fills himself up with. Anyway, lads, pull your chairs up to the table! Katrine, aren't we having any toddy?

MRS STOCKMANN (*heading towards the dining room*). I'm just going to bring it in.

DR STOCKMANN. Sit down here on the settee beside me, Captain Horster – we don't often see you… Please, do sit down, my friends…

The MEN *sit round the table.* MRS STOCKMANN *re-enters, carrying a tray, on which is a kettle, decanters, glasses and suchlike.*

MRS STOCKMANN. There we are – this is arrack, and this one here's rum. And this is cognac… Now, gentlemen – help yourself, please.

DR STOCKMANN (*picking up a glass*). Oh, we'll certainly do that! (*While the toddy is being mixed.*) And let's break out the cigars… Eilif, I think you know where the box is kept. And you can fetch my pipe, Morten.

The BOYS *go out, right.*

I have a sneaking suspicion that Eilif pinches the odd cigar now and again, but I don't let on. (*Calls.*) Oh, and Morten – bring my smoking cap as well! Katrine, can you tell him where I've left it? Ah, he's got it.

The BOYS *bring the various objects in.*

Now, my friends, help yourselves. I'll stick to my pipe. This one's seen me through a lot of rough weather, up there in the frozen north. (*Clinking glasses.*) Your good health! Ah, it's a lot better sitting here, I can tell you, snug and warm.

MRS STOCKMANN (*sits down and begins to knit*). Are you going to sea again soon, Captain Horster?

HORSTER. We'll be ready to sail next week, I think.

MRS STOCKMANN. And you're going to America?

HORSTER. Yes, that's the intention.

BILLING. So you won't be able to vote in the municipal election?

HORSTER. What, there's an election coming up?

BILLING. You mean you don't know?

HORSTER. No, I don't take much interest in these things.

BILLING. But you *are* interested in public affairs, I assume?

HORSTER. No, I don't know the first thing about them.

BILLING. That doesn't matter – you still ought to vote.

HORSTER. What, people who know nothing about them, too?

BILLING. Know nothing? Now, what exactly do you mean by that? Society's like a ship – every man has to take a turn at the wheel.

HORSTER. That principle might hold good on dry land, but it isn't worth much at sea.

HOVSTAD. You know, it's strange how little most seafaring folk seem to care about what happens on land.

BILLING. Quite remarkable.

DR STOCKMANN. Sailors are like birds of passage. They feel at home anywhere, north or south, it doesn't matter. But that's why the rest of us have to be even more active, Mr Hovstad. So, is there anything of interest in tomorrow's *Courier*?

HOVSTAD. Nothing about municipal affairs, no, but I thought I might run that article of yours the day after tomorrow.

DR STOCKMANN. Oh, God, yes – that article! Listen, you'd better hold it over for a bit.

HOVSTAD. Really? But we've got just the right space for it, and I think this is the ideal time…

DR STOCKMANN. Yes, yes, I'm sure you're right, but you'll have to wait all the same. I'll explain later…

PETRA, *wearing a hat and cape, and carrying a pile of exercise books under her arm, comes in from the hall.*

PETRA. Good evening.

DR STOCKMANN. Is that you, Petra? Good evening.

PETRA *exchanges greetings with everyone, then sets down her exercise books on a chair by the door.*

PETRA. And you've all been sitting here enjoying yourselves, while I've been working like a slave.

DR STOCKMANN. Well, you can enjoy yourself now too.

BILLING. Shall I fix you a little glass of toddy?

PETRA (*going up to the table*). No, thanks – I'd rather do it myself. You always make it too strong. Oh, I nearly forgot, Father – I have a letter for you. (*Goes back to the chair where her things are lying.*)

DR STOCKMANN. A letter? From whom?

PETRA (*searching in her coat pocket*). The postman handed it to me just as I was going out…

DR STOCKMANN (*stands up and goes over to her*). And you're only bringing it to me now?

PETRA. I honestly hadn't time to run back in again. Anyway, here it is.

DR STOCKMANN (*seizing the letter*). Let me see, let me see it, child. (*Looks at the address.*) Yes, this is it!

MRS STOCKMANN. Is that the one you've been waiting for, Tomas?

DR STOCKMANN. It is indeed. I'd better go right away and… Now, where'll I find a light, Katrine? Is there no lamp in my study yet?

MRS STOCKMANN. The lamp's lit, and it's standing on your desk.

DR STOCKMANN. Good, good. If you'll excuse me for a second… (*Goes into the room at right.*)

PETRA. What d'you think it can be, Mother?

MRS STOCKMANN. I've no idea. The past few days he's done nothing but ask if the postman's been yet.

BILLING. It's probably from one of his out-of-town patients…

PETRA. Poor Father! He really does take on too much work. (*Mixing her toddy.*) Mm… this'll be nice.

HOVSTAD. Have you been teaching an evening class again?

PETRA (*sipping her toddy*). Two hours.

BILLING. And four hours in the mornings at the Institute…

PETRA (*sits down at the table*). Five hours.

MRS STOCKMANN. And essays to correct this evening, I see.

PETRA. A whole stack, yes.

HORSTER. So it looks as if you have plenty to keep you busy too.

PETRA. Yes, but I enjoy it. You feel so deliciously tired afterwards.

BILLING. And you like that?

PETRA. Yes, I do – you get such a good sleep.

MORTEN. You must be very wicked, Petra.

PETRA. Wicked?

MORTEN. Because you work so hard. Mr Rørlund says that work is a punishment for our sins.

EILIF. Pah! You must be very stupid to believe a thing like that.

MRS STOCKMANN. Now, now, Eilif!

BILLING (*laughs*). Oh, that's excellent!

HOVSTAD. Wouldn't you like to work so hard, Morten?

MORTEN. I certainly would not.

HOVSTAD. So, what do you want to be when you grow up?

MORTEN. I'd like to be a Viking.

EILIF. That means you'd have to be a heathen.

MORTEN. Fine, I'll be a heathen.

BILLING. Well, I'm on your side, Morten – that's exactly what I say.

MRS STOCKMANN (*making signs*). I'm sure you do nothing of the kind, Mr Billing.

BILLING. God damn it, I *am* a heathen, and proud of it! Just wait, we'll all be heathens soon enough.

MORTEN. And then we'll be able to do whatever we like, won't we?

BILLING. Well, you see, Morten…

MRS STOCKMANN. Now, off you go, boys – I'm sure you've got some homework to do for tomorrow.

EILIF. I can stay a bit longer, can't I?

MRS STOCKMANN. No, you can't. Now, off you go, both of you.

The BOYS *say goodnight and go into the room at left.*

HOVSTAD. D'you really think it's harmful for the boys to hear these things?

MRS STOCKMANN. I don't know, but I'm not happy about it.

PETRA. Well, I think you're wrong there, Mother.

MRS STOCKMANN. Yes, that may well be, but I don't like it. Not at home.

PETRA. You know, there's so much hypocrisy, both at home and at school. At home, we have to keep quiet, and at school, we have to tell the children lies.

HORSTER. Tell them lies?

PETRA. Oh, yes. What, you don't think we have to teach them all sorts of things we don't believe in ourselves?

BILLING. That's true, for a start.

PETRA. And if I had the money, I'd set up a school of my own – an entirely different kind of school.

BILLING. Huh, money!

HORSTER. Well, if that's your plan, Miss Stockmann, I'll gladly let you have some accommodation. My late father's old house is enormous, and it's more or less lying empty. There's a huge dining room on the ground floor...

PETRA (*laughs*). Yes, thank you very much, but I'm afraid it's not likely to come to anything.

HOVSTAD. No, I think Miss Petra's much more likely to go into journalism. Incidentally, have you had time to look over that English story you said you'd translate for us?

PETRA. No, not yet, but you'll have it in good time, I promise.

DR STOCKMANN *comes in from his study, the open letter in his hand.*

DR STOCKMANN *(waving the letter)*. Now, just wait till the town gets to hear this news!

BILLING. News?

MRS STOCKMANN. What news?

DR STOCKMANN. A great discovery, Katrine!

HOVSTAD. Really?

MRS STOCKMANN. Which you've made?

DR STOCKMANN. Which I've made, yes. *(Begins pacing to and fro.)* Well, let them come now, the way they always do, and say it's all just the wild imaginings of some lunatic. But they'd better watch out. *(Laughs.)* Yes, indeed, they'll change their tune this time!

PETRA. But, Father, tell us what it is.

DR STOCKMANN. Yes, yes, just bear with me, and you'll soon know the whole story. Oh, if only I had Peter here now! This just shows how we humans can go around passing judgements, yet we're as blind as moles.

HOVSTAD. What do you mean, doctor?

DR STOCKMANN *(coming to a halt by the table)*. Well, isn't it generally understood that our town is a healthy place?

HOVSTAD. Why, yes, of course.

DR STOCKMANN. A quite exceptionally healthy place – a place, moreover, highly recommended for sick and healthy people alike...

MRS STOCKMANN. Yes, but, Tomas dear...

DR STOCKMANN. And we ourselves have recommended it, and sung its praises. I've written screeds about it in the *Courier*, and in various brochures...

HOVSTAD. Yes? So?

DR STOCKMANN. And about its municipal Baths, what they call the very pulse of the town, its nerve centre, and God knows what other names they have for it...

BILLING. 'The town's beating heart', I was moved to call it once, on some solemn occasion or other.

DR STOCKMANN. Yes, well, that too. But do you know what it is in reality – this great and glorious, highly praised establishment, which has cost us so much money? Do you know what it is?

HOVSTAD. No, what is it?

MRS STOCKMANN. Yes, what is it?

DR STOCKMANN. A cesspool – the whole place is a cesspool.

PETRA. The Baths, Father!

MRS STOCKMANN (*simultaneously*). Our Baths!

HOVSTAD (*likewise*). But, doctor...

BILLING. Absolutely incredible!

DR STOCKMANN. The entire Baths complex is polluted, I tell you, a toxic whited sepulchre. A positive health hazard, unsanitary in the extreme! All that filth up at Mølledal, where there's such a vile stench – it's been leaking into the pipes that feed the pump room – and that same damned poisonous sludge is spilling onto the beach as well…

HORSTER. You mean at the bathing area?

DR STOCKMANN. Precisely.

HOVSTAD. What makes you so sure of all this, doctor?

DR STOCKMANN. I've taken great pains to research the matter, to the best of my ability. Oh, I've had my suspicions for quite some time now. Last year, for example, there were a number of unusual cases among visitors to the Baths – typhoid, and gastric fever…

MRS STOCKMANN. Yes, so there were.

DR STOCKMANN. At that time we assumed it was the tourists who had brought these infections in with them. But over the course of the winter I began to have second thoughts, so I started testing the water, as far as I could.

MRS STOCKMANN. So that's what's been keeping you so busy!

DR STOCKMANN. I've certainly been busy, Katrine, you can say that. But of course I didn't have the necessary scientific equipment here, so I sent test samples of both fresh and seawater to the university for a precise laboratory analysis.

HOVSTAD. And that's what you've just received?

DR STOCKMANN (*waving the letter*). This is it, yes! It provides clear evidence of the presence of decayed organic matter

in the water – millions of bacteria – making it extremely
hazardous to health, for either internal or external use.

MRS STOCKMANN. Thank heavens you've found out
about it in time.

DR STOCKMANN. You may well say that.

HOVSTAD. And what are you planning to do now, doctor?

DR STOCKMANN. Well, naturally, I'm going to see that it's
put right.

HOVSTAD. And can that be done?

DR STOCKMANN. It must be. Otherwise the whole
establishment's useless – the Baths are ruined. But there's
no danger of that – I know exactly what needs to be done.

MRS STOCKMANN. But, Tomas dear, why have you kept
all this so secret?

DR STOCKMANN. Well, I could hardly dash all over the
town spreading the word until I had made absolutely
certain, could I? No, thank you – I'm not that crazy.

PETRA. But not even to us at home…

DR STOCKMANN. Not to a single living soul. But you can
run round to the old Badger tomorrow…

MRS STOCKMANN. Oh, Tomas!

DR STOCKMANN. All right, all right – to your grandfather,
then. Yes, this'll give the old boy something to chew over.
He's always thought I was a bit touched. Oh yes, and I'm
well aware there's quite a few people thinking the same
thing. Well, now all these good folk'll have their eyes
opened, they'll see something this time! (*Walking round,
rubbing his hands.*) This is going to cause quite a stir in the

town, Katrine. You can't imagine it – all the pipes'll have
to be relaid.

HOVSTAD (*stands up*). All the pipes?

DR STOCKMANN. Yes, that goes without saying. The water
intake's too far down, it'll have to be sited much higher up.

PETRA. So you were right all along.

DR STOCKMANN. Ah, you remember that, Petra? I wrote
to them, when they were just starting to build, but nobody
would listen to me. Well, now you can be sure I'm going to
let them have it. Naturally, I've written a report for the
Baths Committee – it's been lying ready a whole week; I
was just waiting for this… (*Holds up the letter.*) Anyway, we'll
post this off immediately. (*Goes into his room and returns with a
sheaf of papers.*) Now, look! Four closely written pages, plus a
covering letter. Katrine, some newspaper! Something – to
wrap this up in. Good, that'll do… now give it to… to…
(*Stamps his foot.*) Oh, God, what's her name again? Give it to
the maid, and tell her to take it straight to the Mayor.

MRS STOCKMANN *takes the packet and goes out through the
dining room.*

PETRA. What do you think Uncle Peter'll say, Father?

DR STOCKMANN. What would you expect him to say?
He'll be delighted, I'm sure, that such an important matter
is being brought to light.

HOVSTAD. And may I have permission to insert a little piece
about your discovery in the *Courier*?

DR STOCKMANN. By all means, I'd be most grateful.

HOVSTAD. The public really ought to know about this, and
the sooner the better.

DR STOCKMANN. Absolutely.

MRS STOCKMANN (*returning*). That's her gone with it now.

BILLING. I swear to God, doctor, you'll be the toast of the town!

DR STOCKMANN (*pacing up and down delightedly*). Oh, nonsense – when you get right down to it, I'm only doing my duty. I've made a lucky find, that's all. Still, even so…

BILLING. Hovstad, don't you think the town should organise a parade in Dr Stockmann's honour?

HOVSTAD. Yes, indeed – I'll put the word about, anyway.

BILLING. And I'll speak to Aslaksen about it.

DR STOCKMANN. No, no, dear friends, that's enough silliness. I don't want any kind of celebration. And if the board should decide to increase my salary, I'll refuse it. I'm telling you now, Katrine, I won't take it.

MRS STOCKMANN. You're doing the right thing, Tomas.

PETRA (*raising her glass*). Your health, Father!

HOVSTAD *and* BILLING. Your health, doctor!

HORSTER (*clinking glasses with him*). Here's wishing you all the very best with it!

DR STOCKMANN. Thank you, thank you, my dearest friends! I'm absolutely overjoyed! It's such a good feeling to know that you've been of service to your own hometown, and your fellow-citizens. Hurrah, Katrine!

He flings his arms around her and whirls about the room with her. She shrieks and struggles to get free. Laughter, applause, and cheering for the DOCTOR. *The* BOYS *pop their heads round the door.*

ACT TWO

The DOCTOR's *living room. The door leading to the dining room is closed. It is morning.* MRS STOCKMANN *enters from the dining room with a sealed letter in her hand, crosses to the first door on the right, and looks in.*

MRS STOCKMANN. Tomas, are you in?

DR STOCKMANN (*from within*). Yes, I just got back. (*Entering.*) Is that something for me?

MRS STOCKMANN. A letter from your brother. (*Hands it to him.*)

DR STOCKMANN. Ah, let's have a look. (*Opens the envelope and reads.*) 'The enclosed manuscript is returned herewith…' (*Reads on in an undertone.*) Hm…

MRS STOCKMANN. So, what does he say?

DR STOCKMANN (*stuffing the papers into his pocket*). Oh, nothing – just that he'll pop in himself around midday.

MRS STOCKMANN. You'd better remember to stay home, then.

DR STOCKMANN. That's no problem – I've finished all my morning calls.

MRS STOCKMANN. I'd really love to know how he's taking all this.

DR STOCKMANN. Well, he won't be happy that I was the one who made the discovery, and not him.

MRS STOCKMANN. Yes, doesn't that bother you a little?

DR STOCKMANN. Oh, deep down he'll be pleased, as you can well imagine, but Peter gets damnably upset if anyone other than himself does something for the town.

MRS STOCKMANN. Actually, Tomas, it would be nice if you could share the honour with him. Couldn't you drop a hint that it was he who put you on the right track?

DR STOCKMANN. I don't mind. Just as long as I can get this business cleared up…

Old MORTEN KIIL *pops his head in at the hall door and looks round inquiringly, with a hint of amusement.*

MORTEN KIIL (*slyly*). So… is it true, then?

MRS STOCKMANN (*going towards him*). Father, it's you!

DR STOCKMANN. Mr Kiil – good morning, sir, good morning!

MRS STOCKMANN. Come in, do.

MORTEN KIIL. Only if it's true – otherwise I'll go away again.

DR STOCKMANN. If what's true?

MORTEN KIIL. This idiotic business about the water supply. It's true, then, is it?

DR STOCKMANN. It certainly is. But how on earth did you hear about it?

MORTEN KIIL (*entering*). Petra dropped in, on her way past to school.

DR STOCKMANN. Oh, did she now?

MORTEN KIIL. She did – she told me the whole story. I thought she was just pulling my leg, but that's not Petra's style.

DR STOCKMANN. No, indeed. So what made you think that?

MORTEN KIIL. You can't trust anybody these days – you can be so easily fooled. Anyway – I take it it *is* true?

DR STOCKMANN. Absolutely. Now do sit down, Father-in-law, and relax. (*Ushers him onto the settee.*) It's a good thing for the town, don't you think?

MORTEN KIIL (*trying not to laugh*). A good thing for the town?

DR STOCKMANN. Yes, a good thing that I made the discovery in time…

MORTEN KIIL (*as before*). Oh, yes, yes! I just never imagined you'd play one of your monkey tricks on your own brother.

DR STOCKMANN. Monkey tricks?

MRS STOCKMANN. Now, Father dear, please…

MORTEN KIIL (*rests his hands and chin on the handle of his stick and winks mischievously at the* DOCTOR). What was it again? Oh, yes… didn't you say something about some sort of creatures getting into the water pipes?

DR STOCKMANN. That's right – yes, bacteria.

MORTEN KIIL. All different sorts, according to Petra – lots of little creatures, a huge number of them.

DR STOCKMANN. Yes, indeed – hundreds of thousands of them.

MORTEN KIIL. Only nobody can see them, isn't that so?

DR STOCKMANN. Nobody can see them, that's true.

MORTEN KIIL (*chuckling quietly to himself*). I'll be damned – this is the best you've come up with yet!

DR STOCKMANN. Why? What do you mean?

MORTEN KIIL. You'll never get the Mayor to swallow that.

DR STOCKMANN. Well, we'll see, shall we?

MORTEN KIIL. What, you really think he's that crazy?

DR STOCKMANN. I hope the whole town'll be that crazy.

MORTEN KIIL. The whole town! Oh, yes, that's highly likely. They're quite capable of that, and serve them right. Yes, they think they're so much smarter than us old folks. They hounded me out of the town council – treated me like a dog, I'm telling you. Well, now it's their turn – yes, you go right ahead with your monkey tricks, Stockmann – put one over on them.

DR STOCKMANN. Yes, but...

MORTEN KIIL. One of your monkey tricks, that's all I ask. (*Stands up.*) If you can manage to give the Mayor and his cronies a bloody nose, I'll donate a hundred crowns to charity right on the spot!

DR STOCKMANN. That's very kind of you.

MORTEN KIIL. Yes, well, I don't have money to burn, for sure, but if you can do that, I'll give another fifty crowns to charity next Christmas.

HOVSTAD *enters from the hall.*

HOVSTAD. Good morning! (*Stops.*) Oh, I beg your pardon...

DR STOCKMANN. No, come in, come in, please.

MORTEN KIIL *(chuckles again)*. Him! Is he in on it too?

HOVSTAD. What do you mean?

DR STOCKMANN. Yes, of course he's in on it.

MORTEN KIIL. I might have known! It's got to go into the papers. Well, if you aren't the limit, Stockmann. Just put one over on them, that's all. Anyway, I'll leave you to it.

DR STOCKMANN. No, no – stay a little while, Father-in-law.

MORTEN KIIL. No, I'd better be going. Now, you mind and throw every trick in the book at them. Damn it, man, you'll be doing yourself a good turn.

Goes out, accompanied by MRS STOCKMANN.

DR STOCKMANN *(laughs)*. Would you credit it? The old man doesn't believe a word of this business with the water system.

HOVSTAD. Oh, is *that* what you…?

DR STOCKMANN. That's what we were talking about, yes. And no doubt you're here for the same reason?

HOVSTAD. Yes, I am. Have you a spare minute, doctor?

DR STOCKMANN. All the time you want, my dear friend.

HOVSTAD. Have you heard anything from the Mayor yet?

DR STOCKMANN. Not yet. He'll be dropping in later.

HOVSTAD. I've been giving this business a good deal of thought since yesterday evening.

DR STOCKMANN. And?

HOVSTAD. Well, for you as a doctor, and as a scientist, this water-pipes situation is something in its own right. I mean, it doesn't seem to have occurred to you that it's actually tied in to a great many other things.

DR STOCKMANN. Oh, in what way? Let's sit down, my dear friend – over there, on the settee…

HOVSTAD *sits down on the settee, and the* DOCTOR *in an armchair at the other side of the table.*

Now – you were saying… ?

HOVSTAD. Well, you were talking yesterday about the water being polluted by impurities in the soil.

DR STOCKMANN. Yes, and without a shadow of doubt it's coming from that poisoned swamp up at Mølledal.

HOVSTAD. If you'll forgive me, doctor, I think it comes from a very different swamp.

DR STOCKMANN. Oh, and what swamp is this?

HOVSTAD. The swamp our whole community stands in, slowly rotting.

DR STOCKMANN. What the devil is that supposed to mean, Mr Hovstad?

HOVSTAD. Bit by bit, every activity in the town has fallen into the hands of a little clique of bureaucrats…

DR STOCKMANN. Oh, come, they're not all bureaucrats.

HOVSTAD. No, well, those who aren't are their cronies and hangers-on – all the rich folk of the town, the same old names. These are the people who control our lives, the ones with the power.

DR STOCKMANN. Yes, but these are people of proven ability and insight.

HOVSTAD. And did they demonstrate ability and insight when they opted to lay the water pipes where they are now?

DR STOCKMANN. No, that was frankly very stupid of them. But we're going to remedy that.

HOVSTAD. And you think that'll all be plain sailing?

DR STOCKMANN. Plain sailing or no, it'll have to go ahead.

HOVSTAD. Yes, especially if the press gets involved.

DR STOCKMANN. That won't be necessary, my dear friend. I'm sure my brother…

HOVSTAD. Forgive me, doctor, but I have to tell you that I'm planning to take this issue up.

DR STOCKMANN. In the paper?

HOVSTAD. Yes, when I took over at the *Courier*, it was with the intention of breaking up this ring of pig-headed old fogeys who held all the power.

DR STOCKMANN. But you yourself told me what happened – you very nearly ruined the paper.

HOVSTAD. Yes, well, we had to draw our horns in on that occasion, that's quite true. That was because there was some risk that the whole business of establishing the Baths might have come to nothing, if these people had been removed from power. But we've got the Baths now, so these fine gentlemen are expendable.

DR STOCKMANN. Expendable, yes, perhaps, but we still owe them a debt of gratitude.

HOVSTAD. And that'll be acknowledged too, in all justice. But a journalist of my radical persuasion simply can't let an opportunity like this slip by. We have to destroy the myth of the infallibility of the ruling elite. That kind of thing has to be rooted out, like any other superstition.

DR STOCKMANN. Now, there I wholeheartedly agree with you, Mr Hovstad – if it's a superstition, away with it!

HOVSTAD. Of course, I'm rather loath to implicate the Mayor, since he *is* your brother. But I'm sure you'll agree with me that the truth comes first, before any other consideration.

DR STOCKMANN. That goes without saying. (*With sudden vehemence.*) Yes, but… but…!

HOVSTAD. You mustn't think badly of me. I'm no more self-seeking or ambitious than the next man.

DR STOCKMANN. But, my dear fellow, whoever suggested you were?

HOVSTAD. I come from a poor family, as you know. So I've had plenty of opportunity to observe what the lower orders most urgently need, and it's this, doctor: to be able to play some part in the direction of public affairs. That's what will truly develop a man's ability, knowledge, and confidence in himself…

DR STOCKMANN. That I can well understand…

HOVSTAD. Yes, so it's my feeling that a journalist must bear an awesome responsibility if he chooses to neglect any opportunity to emancipate the people, the humble, downtrodden masses. Oh, I'm well aware the rich folk are going to call this rabble-rousing, and so forth, but they can say what they like. Just as long as my conscience is clear…

DR STOCKMANN. Absolutely! That's so true, my dear Hovstad. But all the same… I mean, damn it, really…!

A knock at the door.

Come in!

The printer ASLAKSEN appears in the hall doorway. He is humbly but respectably dressed in black, with a slightly crumpled white cravat, and holding gloves and a stovepipe hat in his hand.

ASLAKSEN (*bowing*). Excuse me, doctor, for taking the liberty…

DR STOCKMANN (*rising*). Well, well, if it isn't our printer, Mr Aslaksen!

ASLAKSEN. That's right, doctor.

HOVSTAD (*stands up*). Is it me you're looking for, Aslaksen?

ASLAKSEN. No, sir, it isn't. I didn't know I'd find you here. No, it's the doctor himself I wanted…

DR STOCKMANN. So, what can I do for you?

ASLAKSEN. Is it true, sir, what Mr Billing tells me, that the doctor is thinking about improving our water system?

DR STOCKMANN. To the Baths, yes.

ASLAKSEN. I see. Well, now I know for sure, I've just come to tell you that the project will have my full support.

HOVSTAD (*to the DOCTOR*). There – you see?

DR STOCKMANN. Well, thank you, I'm most grateful, but…

ASLAKSEN. Because you might well need our backing – us small-businesspeople, I mean. We make up a pretty solid majority in this town – that is, when we really *want* to. And it's always a good thing to have the majority on your side, doctor.

DR STOCKMANN. That's undoubtedly true. But I scarcely imagine that all these special measures are going to be necessary here. I mean, such a simple, straightforward business…

ASLAKSEN. Oh yes, but it might be a good idea just the same. You see, I know these local authorities extremely well. And the people at the top don't take kindly to suggestions coming from outsiders. That's why I think it wouldn't be a bad thing if we organised some sort of little demonstration.

HOVSTAD. That's right.

DR STOCKMANN. A demonstration, you say? So how exactly do you plan to demonstrate?

ASLAKSEN. Oh, with the utmost moderation, doctor, of course – I'm a firm believer in moderation, in all things. It's a citizen's greatest virtue – that's *my* opinion, at any rate.

DR STOCKMANN. Indeed, Mr Aslaksen, you have that reputation.

ASLAKSEN. Yes, I think I can safely say that. And this matter of the water supply – it's hugely important for us small businessmen. The Baths show every sign of becoming a bit of a gold mine for the town. We'll all make a living out of them, especially those of us who are homeowners. That's why we're willing to support this

project every way we can. I'm speaking now as the
chairman of the Homeowners' Association...

DR STOCKMANN. Yes?

ASLAKSEN. And I happen also to represent the local
Temperance Society – the doctor is no doubt aware that
I'm very active in the Temperance movement.

DR STOCKMANN. Why, yes, of course.

ASLAKSEN. So you'll understand that I come into contact
with a great many people. And since I do have the
reputation of being a sober and law-abiding citizen, as you
yourself have said, doctor, it means I have a certain
amount of influence in the town – a little bit of power, if I
may be allowed to say so.

DR STOCKMANN. Yes, I'm well aware of that, Mr
Aslaksen.

ASLAKSEN. So you see, it would be quite a simple matter for
me to work up a testimonial, if that should be deemed
necessary.

DR STOCKMANN. A testimonial?

ASLAKSEN. Yes, a sort of vote of thanks from the townsfolk
in recognition of the way you've tackled this important civic
issue. It goes without saying that it must be drawn up with
the utmost moderation, so as not to offend the authorities,
and the people in power. And provided we are careful in
that respect, I don't think anyone will object, do you?

HOVSTAD. Well, even supposing they didn't like it...

ASLAKSEN. No, no, no – we don't want any show of
hostility towards the authorities, Mr Hovstad. No

confrontation with people who have so much control over
our lives. I've had enough of that in my time, and no good
ever comes of it. But I'm sure nobody can take exception
to the reasonable expression of a man's honest opinion.

DR STOCKMANN (*shakes his hand*). My dear Mr Aslaksen, I
can't tell you how happy I am to find so much support
among my fellow-citizens. I'm delighted, positively delighted!
Now, you'll take a little drop of sherry, won't you? Eh?

ASLAKSEN. Oh, no, thank you. I don't touch any kind of
spirits.

DR STOCKMANN. Well, a glass of beer, then – what do you
say?

ASLAKSEN. No, thank you again, doctor – I never drink this
early in the day. Anyway, I'm going into town now to have
a word with some of the homeowners, and prepare the
ground.

DR STOCKMANN. This is extraordinarily kind of you, Mr
Aslaksen, but I wouldn't have imagined that all these
measures were necessary. I'd have thought this business
could well look after itself.

ASLAKSEN. I'm afraid the authorities are rather slow to
action, doctor. Not that I'm pointing the finger at anybody
– no, heaven forbid!

HOVSTAD. We'll go after them in the paper tomorrow,
Aslaksen.

ASLAKSEN. But no expressions of violence, please, Mr
Hovstad. Go about it with moderation, or you'll get
nowhere. You can take my word for it, because I've
gleaned my experience from the school of life. Well, I'll say

goodbye now, doctor. And you know that we small businessmen now stand behind you, like a brick wall. Yes, you have that solid majority on your side, doctor.

DR STOCKMANN. Well, thank you very much, my dear Mr Aslaksen. (*Holds out his hand.*) Goodbye, goodbye.

ASLAKSEN. Are you coming with me to the print shop, Mr Hovstad?

HOVSTAD. I'll be along in a minute, I've a couple of things still to do.

ASLAKSEN. Good, good.

He bows and goes out. DR STOCKMANN *accompanies him into the hall.*

HOVSTAD (*when the* DOCTOR *returns*). Well, now, doctor, what do you say to that? Don't you think it's time we had a real shake-up, and let some air into this town, clear out all that gutless, weak-kneed inertia?

DR STOCKMANN. Are you referring to Mr Aslaksen?

HOVSTAD. Yes, I am. He's one of those people stuck in the swamp – though he's a decent enough fellow in other respects. That's what most of them are like around here – they stumble along, see-sawing from one side to another, so guarded and scrupulous that they never take any kind of decisive step.

DR STOCKMANN. Yes, but Aslaksen did seem genuinely well-intentioned.

HOVSTAD. Well, there's something I rate higher, and that's standing your ground, like a man with a bit of confidence in himself.

DR STOCKMANN. Yes, you're absolutely right there.

HOVSTAD. That's why I want to take this opportunity now, to see if I can't force these well-intentioned people to behave like real men for once. This blind worship of authority has got to be rooted out in this town. And this gross, unpardonable error of judgement about the water system needs to be exposed, and brought home to every voter.

DR STOCKMANN. Good – if you think that's in the public interest, so be it. Only not before I've spoken with my brother, please.

HOVSTAD. Well, I'll write my editorial and have it ready, anyway. And if the Mayor refuses to take the matter up…

DR STOCKMANN. Oh, come – what makes you think he won't?

HOVSTAD. It's not inconceivable. And if he doesn't…?

DR STOCKMANN. Well, in that event, I promise you… Listen, in that event, you have my permission to publish my report, verbatim and in full.

HOVSTAD. May I do that? I have your word?

DR STOCKMANN (*hands him the manuscript*). Here, you can have it – take it with you. It'll do no harm if you read it through, and you can give it back to me later.

HOVSTAD. Good, I'll do that. So, goodbye, doctor.

DR STOCKMANN. Goodbye, goodbye! Yes, you'll see, Mr Hovstad – it'll all go like clockwork. Yes, indeed – like clockwork!

HOVSTAD. Hm… we'll see. (*Bows and goes out through the hall door.*)

DR STOCKMANN (*goes over to the dining room and looks in*). Katrine? Oh, you're back home, Petra?

PETRA (*enters*). Yes, I've just come from school.

MRS STOCKMANN (*enters*). Hasn't he arrived yet?

DR STOCKMANN. Peter? No. But I've had a long chat with Hovstad. He's really quite excited about this discovery I've made. Yes, it seems it's got much wider repercussions than I'd at first imagined. So he's put his newspaper at my disposal, if it should be needed.

MRS STOCKMANN. What, d'you think it *will* be needed?

DR STOCKMANN. No, of course not. But even so, it's a source of pride to know that you have the independent liberal press on your side. Oh, and would you believe it? I've also had a visit from the chairman of the Homeowners' Association.

MRS STOCKMANN. Really? And what was he wanting?

DR STOCKMANN. To offer his support as well. They're all going to back me up, if need be. D'you know what I've got behind me, Katrine?

MRS STOCKMANN. Behind you? No, what's behind you?

DR STOCKMANN. The solid majority.

MRS STOCKMANN. And that's a good thing, is it, Tomas?

DR STOCKMANN. Yes, I should jolly well think so! (*Paces up and down, rubbing his hands.*) Good Lord, yes – it's a wonderful feeling to stand side by side, like brothers-in-arms, with your fellow-citizens!

PETRA. And to be doing such genuinely useful work, Father.

DR STOCKMANN. Yes, and for the benefit of one's own hometown, besides.

MRS STOCKMANN. That's the bell.

DR STOCKMANN. That'll be him now.

A knock at the door.

Come in!

MAYOR (*enters from the hall*). Good morning.

DR STOCKMANN. Peter, good to see you!

MRS STOCKMANN. Good morning, Peter. How are things?

MAYOR. Oh, so-so, thank you. (*To the* DOCTOR.) I received your report yesterday, after office hours, concerning the state of the water supply to the Baths.

DR STOCKMANN. Yes. Have you read it?

MAYOR. Yes, I have.

DR STOCKMANN. And what have you got to say about it?

MAYOR (*with a sidelong glance*). Hm…

MRS STOCKMANN. Come along, Petra.

She and PETRA *go out into the room at left.*

MAYOR (*after a pause*). Was it really necessary to proceed with all these investigations behind my back?

DR STOCKMANN. Well, yes, because until I had absolute proof…

MAYOR. And now you have it, you think?

DR STOCKMANN. Yes, surely you're convinced of that yourself?

MAYOR. And is it your intention to submit this document to the Baths Committee in the form of an official report?

DR STOCKMANN. Yes, it is indeed. Something needs to be done about this matter, and quickly.

MAYOR. You use some rather strong language in your report, as is your custom. Among other things, for example, you say that what we're offering our visitors to the Baths is a permanent case of poisoning.

DR STOCKMANN. Well, Peter, how else would you describe it? I mean, you have to understand – the water's poisonous for both internal and external use. And that's what we're giving to all those poor sick people, who come to us in good faith, and pay through the nose to get their health back!

MAYOR. And then you arrive at the conclusion, by your way of thinking, that we must build a sewer, to drain off these alleged impurities from Mølledal, and that the existing water pipes need to be relaid.

DR STOCKMANN. Well, do you know of any other solution? I certainly don't.

MAYOR. I looked in on the town engineer this morning on some pretext or other, and happened to broach the subject with him, half-joking, and suggested these proposals of yours as something we might consider, under advisement, at some future date.

DR STOCKMANN. Some future date?

MAYOR. He actually smiled at what he took to be a flight of fancy on my part, of course. Have you taken the trouble to work out how much all these proposed alterations would cost? According to the information I received, the total expenditure, in all probability, would be upwards of several hundred thousand crowns.

DR STOCKMANN. As much as that?

MAYOR. Yes. And that's not the worst part. The work would extend over at least two years.

DR STOCKMANN. Two years, you say? Two full years?

MAYOR. At least. And what do we do with the Baths meantime? Close them? Yes, because that's what we'll have to do. Or do you seriously believe people would be willing to travel all this way, if word got out that the water here was injurious to health?

DR STOCKMANN. But that's exactly what it *is*, Peter.

MAYOR. And all this just at the point when the Baths were beginning to make a name for themselves. You know, other towns in the area with the same resources could equally well be developed as health resorts. Don't you think they'll jump at the chance to divert the entire flow of tourist traffic their way? Of course they would, beyond a shadow of doubt. And we'd be left empty-handed, with all that expensive plant. We'd probably have to abandon the project altogether, and you'd be responsible for plunging your hometown into ruin.

DR STOCKMANN. Me? Ruin?

MAYOR. The simple fact is that it's only through the Baths that this town has any future worth the name. You can see that as well as I can.

DR STOCKMANN. So what do you think should be done?

MAYOR. I'm not entirely convinced by your report that the condition of the water supply to the Baths is as serious as you make out.

DR STOCKMANN. Actually, it's worse. Or it will be by the summer, when the warm weather arrives.

MAYOR. As I've said, I think you're exaggerating rather. Any competent physician should know what measures to take – he should be able to prevent any harmful effects occurring, or at least treat them, if their presence were to become obvious.

DR STOCKMANN. And then? What next?

MAYOR. Well, the existing water supply to the Baths is a fait accompli, and must be accepted as such. However, the Baths Committee will most likely take your report on board, and won't be averse to discussing to what extent – bearing in mind financial considerations, of course – certain improvements might be instituted.

DR STOCKMANN. And what makes you think I'd have anything to do with that kind of deception?

MAYOR. Deception?

DR STOCKMANN. Deception, yes, that's what it would be – a fraud, a lie, an out-and-out crime perpetrated against the public and the whole of society.

MAYOR. As I've already said, I'm afraid I haven't been able to convince myself that there's any real imminent danger here.

DR STOCKMANN. Oh yes, you have! There's no alternative. My report is absolutely accurate and conclusive, I know it.

And you know it too, Peter, but you won't admit it. You
were the one who insisted on having the Baths and the
water supply sited where they are now. And it's *this* – this
hellish blunder of yours that you won't admit to! Hah! Do
you think I can't see right through you?

MAYOR. And even if that were true? Even if I *do* appear to
be guarding my own reputation a little too jealously, it's all
for the benefit of the town. Without some degree of moral
authority I wouldn't be able to direct the town's affairs in
the way I adjudge to be in the best interests of the
community. That's why – among various other reasons – it
strikes me as imperative that your report shouldn't be
handed over to the Baths Committee. I'll table the matter
for discussion at some later point, and we'll do what we can
in private, but until then, nothing – not a single word about
this disastrous affair – must be made public.

DR STOCKMANN. Well, my dear Peter, I don't think that
can be prevented now.

MAYOR. It must be – it *will* be prevented.

DR STOCKMANN. It's no use, I'm telling you – too many
people know already.

MAYOR. Know already? Who? Surely not those fellows on
the *Courier*?

DR STOCKMANN. Yes, them – of course they know. The
independent liberal press'll make sure you do your duty.

MAYOR (*after a brief pause*). You're an extremely reckless man,
Tomas. Haven't you given any thought to the consequences
this might have for yourself?

DR STOCKMANN. Consequences? For me?

MAYOR. You and your family, yes.

DR STOCKMANN. What the devil do you mean by *that*?

MAYOR. Over the years, I think I can say I've always been an obliging and devoted brother to you.

DR STOCKMANN. You have indeed – and I'm grateful for it.

MAYOR. Oh, I don't want gratitude. To some extent I needed to be, for my own sake. You see, I always hoped that by helping you to improve your financial position, I could exercise a certain degree of control over you.

DR STOCKMANN. What? You mean you did it for your own sake?

MAYOR. To some extent, I said. It's frankly embarrassing for a public servant to have his closest relative compromising himself time and time again.

DR STOCKMANN. You think that's what I do?

MAYOR. Yes, sad to say, you do, without even realising it. You have a restless, aggressive, rebellious temperament. And moreover an unfortunate tendency to rush into print on all manner of subjects. No sooner does an idea come into your head, but you've instantly got to write a newspaper article, or even a whole pamphlet about it.

DR STOCKMANN. Yes, but if he hits on a genuinely new idea, isn't it a citizen's duty to share it with the general public?

MAYOR. The public doesn't need new ideas. The public is best served by the good old, time-honoured ideas it already possesses.

DR STOCKMANN. Well, that's plain speaking, I must say!

MAYOR. Yes, I need to speak to you plainly for once. Up till
now I've tried to avoid that, because I know how irritable
you can be, but I'm going to tell you the truth now, Tomas.
You really have no idea how much harm you do to yourself
with this headstrong behaviour. You complain about the
authorities – yes, even about the government. You're
forever sniping at them, claiming you've been passed over,
and persecuted. But what can you expect, when you're
such a difficult customer?

DR STOCKMANN. So I'm difficult now?

MAYOR. Yes, Tomas, you're an extremely difficult person to
deal with. I know that from experience. You show
absolutely no consideration for other people, and you seem
to forget that it's me you have to thank for your position
here as the Baths medical officer...

DR STOCKMANN. I was the obvious choice. No one but
me, and me alone! I was the first to see that this town could
become a flourishing spa. And at that time, I was the only
one who *could* see it. I had to fight single-handedly for that
idea, year after year, writing non-stop...

MAYOR. Undoubtedly. But it wasn't the right moment then.
And of course that was something you couldn't judge,
stuck up there in the back of beyond. However, as soon the
opportune moment *did* arrive, I – along with a few other
people – took the matter in hand...

DR STOCKMANN. Yes, and made a complete mess of my
excellent scheme. Oh, yes, it's patently obvious now, isn't it,
what a clever lot you were!

MAYOR. The only thing that's obvious to me, I'm afraid, is
that you're hell-bent on starting another argument. You
have to find an outlet for your spleen, so you attack your

superiors – it's the same old story. You can't stand any kind of authority, you're deeply suspicious of anyone in a higher official position – you regard them as a personal enemy, and any weapon that comes to hand will do. But now I've called your attention to the interests that are at stake here – those of the whole town, and in consequence also my own – I need to warn you, Tomas, that I'll be utterly inflexible, with respect to the demand I'm now about to make of you.

DR STOCKMANN. Demand? What demand?

MAYOR. Well, since you've been so indiscreet as to discuss this delicate situation with certain unauthorised individuals, despite the fact that it should have been a confidential matter for the Baths Committee alone, it can't of course be hushed up now. All kinds of rumours will shortly be flying around, and the malcontents in our midst will be at pains to embellish them with additions of their own. It is therefore imperative that you make a public denial of these rumours.

DR STOCKMANN. Me? How? I don't understand.

MAYOR. What we expect is that upon further investigation you will arrive at the conclusion that the situation isn't nearly as critical or dangerous as you at first imagined.

DR STOCKMANN. Aha! So that's what you expect, is it?

MAYOR. And furthermore, we expect you to make public profession of your support for, and absolute trust in the Baths Committee to take whatever measures may become necessary, with the utmost thoroughness and diligence, to remedy any possible defects.

DR STOCKMANN. Yes, well, you'll never get anywhere by simply tinkering with the problem, applying patchwork solutions. I'm telling you that now, Peter, and that's my considered personal opinion.

MAYOR. As an employee of the Baths, you don't have the right to a separate personal opinion.

DR STOCKMANN (*stands up*). Don't have the right?

MAYOR. As an employee, I'm saying. As a private individual... well, good heavens, that's a different matter. However, as a subordinate official employed by the Baths, you have absolutely no authority to express any opinion which runs contrary to that of your superiors.

DR STOCKMANN. Well, that beats everything! I'm a doctor, a man of science, and I have no right to an opinion?

MAYOR. The point at issue here isn't simply a scientific one – this is a complex affair, involving both technical and economic concerns.

DR STOCKMANN. As far as I'm concerned, it can be what the hell it likes, but I intend to be free to express myself on any subject under the sun!

MAYOR. By all means, do. But not on the subject of the Baths. That we forbid.

DR STOCKMANN (*shouting*). You forbid! You? A bunch of...

MAYOR. Yes, *I* forbid it – I, your superior. And if I forbid it, you have to obey.

DR STOCKMANN (*controlling himself*). Peter – if you weren't my brother...

PETRA (*flinging open the door*). You don't have to put up with this, Father!

MRS STOCKMANN (*following her in*). Petra, Petra!

MAYOR. Aha, listening at the keyhole!

MRS STOCKMANN. You were so talking so loudly, we couldn't help...

PETRA. No, I *was* there, listening.

MAYOR. Well, I'm just as pleased...

DR STOCKMANN (*going up to him*). You were saying something to me about forbidding and obeying...?

MAYOR. I'm afraid you've forced me to take that tone with you.

DR STOCKMANN. So you want me to stand up in public and contradict myself?

MAYOR. We consider it absolutely essential that you make a public statement, along the lines I've already indicated.

DR STOCKMANN. And supposing I don't... obey?

MAYOR. Well, then, we'll issue a statement ourselves, to reassure the public.

DR STOCKMANN. Fine! Then I'll attack you in the newspapers. I'll stand my ground. I'll prove that I'm right, and you're wrong. And what will you do then?

MAYOR. In that case, I'm afraid I won't be able to prevent your dismissal.

DR STOCKMANN. What?

PETRA. Father – dismissal!

MRS STOCKMANN. Dismissal!

MAYOR. Yes, from your post as the Baths medical officer. I'll find myself compelled to have you put on notice immediately, and suspended from any activity relating to the Baths.

DR STOCKMANN. And you'd dare to do that?

MAYOR. You're the one playing daredevil here.

PETRA. Uncle, this is a shameful way to treat a man like my father!

MRS STOCKMANN. Do be quiet, Petra!

MAYOR (*looks at* PETRA). Aha! I see we've already learned to voice our opinions. Yes, of course we have. (*To* MRS STOCKMANN.) Katrine, you're probably the only sensible person in this house. Use whatever influence you possess over your husband, and make him understand what the consequences will be, both for his family, and for...

DR STOCKMANN. My family is nobody's concern but my own!

MAYOR. Both for his family, as I was saying, and for the town he lives in.

DR STOCKMANN. No, I'm the one with the real interests of the town at heart! All I want is to expose deficiencies that are going to come to light sooner or later anyway. Oh yes, I'll show them how much I *do* love my hometown.

MAYOR. So much that you're blindly determined to cut off the town's principal source of revenue.

DR STOCKMANN. That source is poisoned, man! Are you mad? We're making a living here by peddling filth and corruption! The whole of our flourishing community draws its sustenance from a lie!

MAYOR. Fanciful nonsense – or something even worse. Any man who flings around damaging insinuations like that about his own hometown must be regarded as a public enemy!

DR STOCKMANN (*going towards him*). You dare to…!

MRS STOCKMANN (*thrusting herself between them*). Tomas!

PETRA (*seizing her father's arm*). Father, don't!

MAYOR. Well, I'm not waiting here to be assaulted. You've been warned now. Just give some thought to what you owe yourself and your family. Goodbye. (*Goes out.*)

DR STOCKMANN (*pacing up and down*). And I'm supposed to stand for that? In my own house, Katrine! What do you think of that, eh?

MRS STOCKMANN. It *is* disgraceful, Tomas, and ridiculous, really…

PETRA. Oh, if I could just get my hands on that uncle of mine…!

DR STOCKMANN. It's my own fault. I should've taken a stance against them long ago – shown my teeth – bitten back! Calling me a public enemy! Me! Well, I'm not standing for that – no, by God, I'm not!

MRS STOCKMANN. But, Tomas dear, your brother does have the power…

DR STOCKMANN. And I've got *right* on my side!

MRS STOCKMANN. Yes, of course, you have right on your side – but what use is right without might?

PETRA. Oh, Mother – how can you say such a thing?

DR STOCKMANN. So in a free society, it's no use having right on your side, is that it? You're just being silly, Katrine. Anyway, haven't I got the independent liberal press to take the lead – and that solid majority behind me? That's power enough, I should imagine.

MRS STOCKMANN. For goodness' sake, Tomas, you're surely not thinking of…?

DR STOCKMANN. Not thinking of what?

MRS STOCKMANN. Of setting yourself up against your brother.

DR STOCKMANN. Well, what the devil do you want me to do? Give up my position on what's right and true?

PETRA. Yes, that's exactly the point I was going to make.

MRS STOCKMANN. But it won't do a blind bit of good, as you well know. If they won't, they won't, and that's that.

DR STOCKMANN. Oho, Katrine, just give me time – I'll win this war in the end, you wait and see.

MRS STOCKMANN. Yes, and while you're winning the war, you'll lose your job – that's what you'll do.

DR STOCKMANN. Well, at least I'll have done my duty to the people – to society. And he calls me a public enemy, no less!

MRS STOCKMANN. But your duty to your family, Tomas? To us at home? Do you think *that's* doing your duty, to the people you're supposed to provide for?

PETRA. Oh, Mother, don't always think of ourselves first!

MRS STOCKMANN. Yes, that's easy for you to say. You can stand on your own two feet, if need be. But don't forget the boys, Tomas. And give a little thought to ourselves too, to you and me.

DR STOCKMANN. You must be out of your mind, Katrine. If I were such a miserable coward as to go crawling to Peter and those damned cronies of his, how could I ever again enjoy a single moment's happiness?

MRS STOCKMANN. I don't know, but God preserve us from the kind of happiness we'll all enjoy if you go on defying them. You'll be right back where you started – with no job, no guaranteed income. I thought we'd had our fill of that in the old days. Don't forget that, Tomas, and think what's ahead of us.

DR STOCKMANN (*inwardly struggling, clenching his fists*). And this is how these damned bureaucrats can oppress a free man – a man of integrity! Isn't it terrible, Katrine?

MRS STOCKMANN. Yes, they've treated you shamefully, and that's a fact. But, good heavens, people have to put up with so many injustices in this world. There are the boys, Tomas – look at them! What's going to become of them? No, no – you surely haven't the heart to…

EILIF *and* MORTEN *have meanwhile come in with their schoolbooks.*

DR STOCKMANN. The boys…! (*Suddenly resolute again.*) No, I don't care if the whole world falls apart, I'm not kowtowing to anybody. (*Goes towards his study.*)

MRS STOCKMANN (*following him*). Tomas, what are you going to do?

DR STOCKMANN (*at the door*). I want the right to look my sons in the eye, when they've grown up as free men. (*Goes into his room.*)

MRS STOCKMANN (*bursts into tears*). Oh, God help us all!

PETRA. Father's a wonderful man – he'll never give in.

The BOYS, *bewildered, are about to ask what has happened.* PETRA *motions them to be quiet.*

ACT THREE

The editorial office of The People's Courier. *At rear left is the entrance door; at right in the same wall is a glass-panelled door, through which the press-room is visible. In the right wall is another door. In the centre of the room is a large table, strewn with papers, newspapers and books. Downstage left is a window, before which stands a writing desk with a high stool. There are a couple of armchairs positioned by the table, and a few other chairs along the walls. The room is gloomy and depressing, the furniture old, the armchairs stained and torn. In the press-room, a few typesetters can be seen at work, and beyond them, a hand-press is being operated.* HOVSTAD *is sitting at the desk, writing. After a moment,* BILLING *enters from the right, with* DR STOCKMANN's *manuscript in his hand.*

BILLING. Well, I must say…!

HOVSTAD (*writing*). Have you read it right through?

BILLING (*lays the manuscript on the desk*). I certainly have.

HOVSTAD. Hard-hitting stuff, don't you think?

BILLING. Hard? Ye gods, it's dynamite. Every word strikes home, like… what can I say? Like a blow from a sledgehammer.

HOVSTAD. Yes, but it takes more than one blow to knock these people down.

BILLING. That's true, so we'll just keep pounding away, one blow after another, until their whole high-and-mighty edifice collapses. You know, sitting in there reading it, I felt as though I could see the revolution approaching.

HOVSTAD (*turning round*). Ssshh! You don't want Aslaksen to hear.

BILLING (*lowers his voice*). Aslaksen's a coward – he's chicken-livered. The man has no backbone. But you'll get your own way this time, I trust. The doctor's article's definitely going in?

HOVSTAD. Yes, if the Mayor doesn't give in without a fight.

BILLING. That would be a damn nuisance.

HOVSTAD. Anyway, we can turn the situation to account, no matter what happens. If the Mayor won't accept the doctor's proposal, he'll have the middle classes on his back – the Homeowners' Association and all that lot. And if he *does* accept it, he'll find himself at odds with a whole gang of the major shareholders in the Baths, who've been the mainstay of his support up until now.

BILLING. Yes, indeed. It'll cost them a pretty penny, that's for sure.

HOVSTAD. You're damn right, it will. And that'll break the circle, you see, and we'll be able to enlighten the general public, day after day in the paper, as to how totally incompetent the Mayor is, and how all the positions of responsibility in the town – the entire administration, indeed, ought to be handed over to the liberals.

BILLING. That's absolutely true, so help me God! I can see it, I can see it coming – we're on the brink of a revolution!

There is a knock at the door.

HOVSTAD. Ssshh! (*Calls out.*) Come in!

DR STOCKMANN *enters through the door at rear left.*

(*Going to meet him.*) Ah, here's the doctor. Well?

DR STOCKMANN. Go ahead and print, Mr Hovstad!

HOVSTAD. So it's come to that?

BILLING. Hurrah!

DR STOCKMANN. Print away, I say. Yes, it *has* come to that. But now they'll get what they're asking for. There's going to be war in this town, Mr Billing!

BILLING. A fight to the death, I hope. Cut them to pieces, doctor!

DR STOCKMANN. This article's only the beginning. My head's already crammed full of ideas for another four or five articles. Where will I find Aslaksen?

BILLING (*calls into the press-room*). Aslaksen, come out here a minute!

HOVSTAD. Another four or five articles, you say? On the same subject?

DR STOCKMANN. Oh, no – far from it, my dear fellow. No, they're on quite different issues. But they're all linked to this business of the water supply and the sewers. One thing leads to another, you know. It's like when you begin to renovate an old house – it's exactly like that.

BILLING. By God, that's so true. You soon realise you're never going to stop until you've pulled down the whole pile of rubbish.

ASLAKSEN (*from the press-room*). Pulled down what? The doctor's surely not thinking of pulling the Baths down?

HOVSTAD. No, of course not. There's no need for alarm.

DR STOCKMANN. No, this is about something completely different. Now, Mr Hovstad, what've you got to say about my article?

HOVSTAD. I think it's a real masterpiece…

DR STOCKMANN. It is, isn't it. Yes, I'm very pleased with it – extremely pleased.

HOVSTAD. It's so clear and straightforward. And you don't need to be an expert to get the point of it. I've absolutely no doubt you'll have every educated reader on your side.

ASLAKSEN. And all the reasonable people, I hope.

BILLING. Reasonable and unreasonable alike – virtually the whole town, I reckon.

ASLAKSEN. So we'll take a chance and print it?

DR STOCKMANN. Yes, I should think so!

HOVSTAD. It'll go in tomorrow morning.

DR STOCKMANN. Good heavens, yes – we mustn't lose a single day. Now, Mr Aslaksen, there was something I wanted to ask you – you will give this manuscript your personal attention, won't you?

ASLAKSEN. I shall indeed.

DR STOCKMANN. Treat it as if it were gold. No misprints, please – every word is important. I'll look in again later – possibly I could cast an eye over the proofs. Yes, I can't tell you how eager I am to see this thing in print – finally launched…

BILLING. Launched, yes, that's it – like a thunderbolt!

DR STOCKMANN. ... Submitted to the judgement of every thinking man. Oh, you wouldn't believe what I've had to suffer today. Being threatened with this, that and the next thing – they even wanted to deprive me of my most fundamental human rights...

BILLING. What! Your human rights!

DR STOCKMANN. They tried to humiliate me, make a coward of me – wanted me to put my self-interest ahead of my deepest and most sacred convictions...

BILLING. Damn it, that's a bit much.

HOVSTAD. What else would you expect? That lot are capable of anything.

DR STOCKMANN. Well, it's not going to work with me. And they'll see it spelled out in black and white. Because I'll be in *The People's Courier* every single day, lying at anchor, so to speak, bombarding them with one explosive article after another...

ASLAKSEN. Yes, but...

BILLING. Hurrah! It's war! It's war!

DR STOCKMANN. I'll knock them to the ground, I'll crush them, I'll tear down their defences, so every right-thinking person can see, with their own eyes! That's what I'll do!

ASLAKSEN. But do it in moderation, that's all. Fire away, doctor, but in moderation...

BILLING. No, no! Don't spare the dynamite!

DR STOCKMANN (*continues excitedly*). You see, it's no longer just a question of the water supply and the drains. No, the whole of society needs cleaning up, disinfecting...

BILLING. You've never said a truer word!

DR STOCKMANN. We've got to kick all these old fogeys out. And I mean in every walk of life. Yes, that was a real eye-opener for me today, in so many ways. I can't see it all clearly yet, but it'll come to me in time. We need fresh young standard-bearers – that's what we've got to look for, my friends. We must have new men, commanding all our forward positions.

BILLING. Hear, hear!

DR STOCKMANN. As long as we stick together, everything'll go smoothly, I'm sure. Launching the revolution'll be just like sending a ship down the slipway – don't you think so?

HOVSTAD. For my part, I think we now have every prospect of putting the direction of our community where it rightly belongs.

ASLAKSEN. And as long as we proceed with moderation, I can't imagine there'll be any real risk.

DR STOCKMANN. Who the devil cares whether there's any risk or not? Whatever I do, I'll do in the name of truth, and for the sake of my conscience.

HOVSTAD. You're a man who deserves to be supported, doctor.

ASLAKSEN. Yes, there's no denying it – the doctor is a true friend to the town, a genuine public benefactor, he is indeed.

BILLING. By God, Aslaksen, Dr Stockmann is a friend of the people!

ASLAKSEN. I think the Homeowners' Association might even want to use that as a slogan.

DR STOCKMANN (*deeply moved, grasps their hands*). Thank you, thank you, my dear, trusted friends – it's a real comfort to hear you say that. My own brother called me something quite different. Well, by heaven, it'll come back to haunt him, with interest! Anyway, I'd better go now, I've a patient to see, poor devil. But I'll be back, as I said. Now, take good care of that manuscript, Mr Aslaksen, and whatever you do, don't cut any exclamation marks! Put in a few more, if anything! Excellent! Well, goodbye for now – goodbye, goodbye!

Goodbyes said all round, he is escorted to the door, goes out.

HOVSTAD. That man can be extremely useful to us.

ASLAKSEN. Yes, as long as he sticks to this business of the Baths. But if he goes beyond that, it might not be wise to follow him.

HOVSTAD. Hm! That depends entirely on…

BILLING. Oh, you're so damn fearful, Aslaksen.

ASLAKSEN. Fearful? Well, yes – where it concerns the local powers-that-be, I certainly am fearful, Mr Billing, and that's something I've learned in the school of life, let me tell you. But you just put me in real political office, even in opposition to the government itself, and then see if I'm fearful or not.

BILLING. No, I'm sure you wouldn't be, but that's just where you're so inconsistent.

ASLAKSEN. Well, I'm a man of conscience, and that's the whole issue. You can attack the government, you see, without doing any real damage to society, because these people simply shrug it all off. They just carry on regardless. But the local authorities, well, they *can* be kicked out, and then you run the risk of having inexperienced people at the helm, who might do irreparable damage to the interests of homeowners and other individuals.

HOVSTAD. But self-government should be part of a citizen's education – haven't you thought about that?

ASLAKSEN. Mr Hovstad, when a man has a vested interest in something, he can't be expected to think of everything.

HOVSTAD. Well, I hope to God I never have any vested interests!

BILLING. Hear, hear!

ASLAKSEN (*smiles*). Hm! (*Points to the desk.*) You know, that editorial chair of yours used to be occupied by Sheriff Stensgård.

BILLING (*spits*). Pah! That turncoat.

HOVSTAD. Well, I'm no time-server – and never will be.

ASLAKSEN. A politician should never rule anything out, Mr Hovstad. As for you, Mr Billing – I think you'd better draw in your horns a little too, now that you've applied for the post of secretary to the magistrates.

BILLING. Who, me?

HOVSTAD. Is this true, Billing?

BILLING. Well, yes – but you can be pretty damn sure I only did it to annoy the establishment.

ASLAKSEN. Anyway, it's nothing to do with me. But when I'm accused of being cowardly, or inconsistent in my principles, I'd just like to make one thing absolutely clear: the political record of Aslaksen the printer is an open book. I haven't altered my position in any way whatsoever, except perhaps to become more moderate. My heart is still with the people, but I don't mind admitting that my head inclines a little more towards the authorities – the local ones, I mean. (*Goes out to the press-room.*)

BILLING. Well, Hovstad – shouldn't we try and get rid of him?

HOVSTAD. What, do you know of anybody else who's willing to give us our paper and printing costs in advance?

BILLING. It's a damned nuisance that we don't have any working capital.

HOVSTAD (*sitting down at the desk*). Yes, if only we had *that*…

BILLING. What about making an approach to Dr Stockmann?

HOVSTAD (*leafing through some papers*). What use would that be? He doesn't have anything.

BILLING. No, but he's got a good man up his sleeve – old Morten Kiil – the 'Badger', as they call him.

HOVSTAD (*writing*). And what makes you so sure *he* has any money?

BILLING. Oh, he's got money, by God! And some of it's bound to go to the Stockmanns. He'll certainly have to consider making some sort of provision – for the children, at least.

HOVSTAD (*half-turning*). And you're counting on that?

BILLING. Counting on it? No, of course not – I'm not counting on anything.

HOVSTAD. Just as well. And you'd better not count on that secretary's job either, because I can tell you now – you won't get it.

BILLING. D'you think I don't know that? That's precisely what I want – not to get it, I mean. A rejection like that really fires up your fighting spirit – it's like getting a fresh supply of bile, and that's just what's needed in a one-horse town like this, where nothing exciting ever happens.

HOVSTAD (*writing*). Yes, yes, I know.

BILLING. Well, they'll hear from me soon enough! Now I'll go in and write this appeal to the Homeowners' Association. (*Goes into the room at right.*)

HOVSTAD (*sits at his desk, chews at the end of his pen, and says slowly*). Hm… so that's his game…

A knock at the door.

Come in!

PETRA *enters through the door at rear left.*

(*Rises.*) Oh, it's you – what are you doing here?

PETRA. You'll have to excuse me, but…

HOVSTAD (*pulling out an armchair*). Won't you sit down?

PETRA. No, thanks – I've got to go straight back.

HOVSTAD. Is this something to do with your father, perhaps?

PETRA. No, it's to do with *me*. (*Takes a book out of her coat pocket.*) It's that English novel.

HOVSTAD. You're bringing it back? Why?

PETRA. Because I don't feel like translating it.

HOVSTAD. But you promised me, without fail…

PETRA. Yes, well, I hadn't read it at that point. And I'm pretty sure you haven't it read it either.

HOVSTAD. No, of course not – you know I don't speak English. But…

PETRA. No, indeed. That's why I wanted to say you'll have to look round for something else. (*Lays the book down on the table.*) You can't use this for the *Courier.*

HOVSTAD. Why not?

PETRA. Because it runs completely counter to everything you stand for.

HOVSTAD. Well, as far as that's concerned…

PETRA. No, I don't think you understand me. It's all about some sort of supernatural power that watches over the so-called 'good' people of this world, and arranges everything in their lives for the best – at the same time ensuring that all the so-called 'bad' people get their comeuppance.

HOVSTAD. Yes, but that's fine. That's just the sort of thing people want.

PETRA. And is that really what you want to give your readers? You don't believe a word of it yourself. You know perfectly well that's not what happens in the real world.

HOVSTAD. Yes, you're absolutely right, but an editor can't always do what he wants. You often have to bow to public opinion, in minor matters, at any rate. I mean, politics is the most important thing in life – at least, for a newspaper, it is. And if I want to win people round to liberal and progressive ideas, I mustn't frighten them off. When they find this sort of moral fable on the back pages, they're more ready to accept what we print up front. They feel more secure, as it were.

PETRA. Oh, for shame! Surely you wouldn't be so cunning as to set a trap for your readers? You're not a spider.

HOVSTAD (*smiles*). Thank you for thinking so well of me. No – it was actually Billing's idea, not mine.

PETRA. Billing's!

HOVSTAD. Yes – at least, he was talking about it in here just the other day. And in fact it's Billing who's so keen to put this story in. I don't know the book at all.

PETRA. But how could Mr Billing, with his liberal opinions...

HOVSTAD. Oh, he's a complex character, is Billing. I hear he's even applied for a job as secretary to the magistrates.

PETRA. No, I don't believe it, Mr Hovstad. How on earth could he bring himself to do something like that?

HOVSTAD. Well, you'd better ask him.

PETRA. I'd never have thought that of Mr Billing.

HOVSTAD (*stares at her intently*). You wouldn't? Does it come as such a surprise to you?

PETRA. Yes. Or perhaps not. Oh, I honestly don't know.

HOVSTAD. Journalists like us don't amount to much, Miss Stockmann.

PETRA. Do you seriously mean that?

HOVSTAD. It does occur to me, now and again.

PETRA. Oh, yes – in your ordinary day-to-day existence, that I can well understand. But now, when you're involved in such a great cause…

HOVSTAD. This business with your father, you mean?

PETRA. Yes, exactly. I would imagine you must have a sense of being more valuable now than most other men.

HOVSTAD. Yes, I do feel a bit like that today.

PETRA. Of course you do. Oh, what a glorious profession you've chosen! To be a pioneer like this, clearing a path for unwelcome truths, and bold new ideas…! Even just to stand up and fearlessly declare your support for a man who's been so cruelly wronged…

HOVSTAD. Especially when that man so cruelly wronged is… er, I don't quite know how to put this…

PETRA. Because he's so transparently honest and sincere, do you mean?

HOVSTAD (*quietly*). Especially when that man is your father, is what I mean.

PETRA (*suddenly taken aback*). What?

HOVSTAD. Yes, Petra… Miss Petra.

PETRA. And is that what matters to you, first and foremost? Not the actual cause? Not the truth? Not my father's selfless generosity of spirit?

HOVSTAD. Oh, yes, of course – that too.

PETRA. No, thank you, Mr Hovstad! You've given yourself away now. And I'll never be able to trust you again, in anything.

HOVSTAD. How can you be so angry with me, when it's mostly for your own sake?

PETRA. I'm angry with you because you haven't been honest with my father. You talked to him as though the only thing that mattered to you was truth, and the good of society. You've made fools of us both. You're not the man you pretended to be, Mr Hovstad, and for that I'll never forgive you – never!

HOVSTAD. Actually, you shouldn't be so touchy, Miss Petra – least of all right now.

PETRA. What do you mean – not right now?

HOVSTAD. Because your father can't do without my help.

PETRA (*looks him up and down*). So that's the kind of man you are? Huh!

HOVSTAD. No. No, I'm not. I just don't know what came over me. Please, you have to believe me.

PETRA. I know what I have to believe. Goodbye.

ASLAKSEN (*entering from the press-room, hurriedly, and with an air of mystery*). God in Heaven, Mr Hovstad… (*Sees* PETRA.) Oh, this is very awkward…

PETRA. That's your book there – you can give it to someone else. (*Makes her way to the door.*)

HOVSTAD (*following her*). But, Miss Petra…

PETRA. Goodbye. (*Goes out.*)

ASLAKSEN. Mr Hovstad, listen to me!

HOVSTAD. Yes, yes – what is it?

ASLAKSEN. The Mayor's out there in the press-room.

HOVSTAD. The Mayor, you say?

ASLAKSEN. Yes, he wants a word with you. He came in the back way – didn't want to be seen, I presume.

HOVSTAD. I wonder what he's after? No, wait – I'll go… (*Walks over to the press-room door, opens it, and motions the* MAYOR *to enter.*) Keep a lookout, Aslaksen – make sure nobody…

ASLAKSEN. Yes, I know… (*Goes out into the press-room.*)

MAYOR. Well, Mr Hovstad, I don't suppose you were expecting to see me here.

HOVSTAD. No, to be honest, I wasn't.

MAYOR (*looking around him*). You've got yourself pretty comfortably ensconced here, I see. Yes, very nice.

HOVSTAD. Oh…

MAYOR. And now I've dropped in unannounced, as it were, to take up your valuable time.

HOVSTAD. Please do, Mr Mayor – I'm only too happy to be of service. Here, let me take your things. (*Lays the* MAYOR's *cap and stick on a chair.*) Won't you sit down?

MAYOR. Thank you.

The MAYOR *sits down by the table.* HOVSTAD *does likewise.*

I've had a thoroughly disagreeable experience today, Mr Hovstad.

HOVSTAD. Really? Well, of course – you have a great many issues to contend with…

MAYOR. Yes, well, this particular issue concerns the medical officer at the town Baths.

HOVSTAD. What, Dr Stockmann?

MAYOR. He's presented some sort of report to the Baths Committee, alleging a number of supposed defects at the establishment.

HOVSTAD. No – he hasn't, has he?

MAYOR. Yes, didn't he tell you? I thought he said...

HOVSTAD. Oh yes, that's right – he did mention something about...

ASLAKSEN (*entering from the press-room*). I'll need that manuscript now...

HOVSTAD (*angrily*). Hm... It's there on the desk.

ASLAKSEN (*finds it*). Ah, good.

MAYOR. Why, that's it – that's the very...

ASLAKSEN. Yes, that's the doctor's article, Mr Mayor.

HOVSTAD. Oh, so *that's* the thing you were talking about?

MAYOR. The very same, yes. What do you think of it?

HOVSTAD. Well, I'm no expert, and I've only just glanced at it, but...

MAYOR. But you're going to print it?

HOVSTAD. Well, I can't really refuse a man of his standing...

ASLAKSEN. I have no say in what goes into the paper, Mr Mayor.

MAYOR. No, of course not.

ASLAKSEN. I only print what's handed to me.

MAYOR. Quite so.

ASLAKSEN. So, if you'll excuse me… (*Goes towards the press-room.*)

MAYOR. No, wait a moment, Mr Aslaksen. With your permission, Mr Hovstad…?

HOVSTAD. My pleasure, Mr Mayor.

MAYOR. Now, Mr Aslaksen, you're a level-headed and thoughtful sort of man…

ASLAKSEN. I'm pleased you should think so, Mr Mayor.

MAYOR. And a man of some considerable influence in the town.

ASLAKSEN. Well, mainly among the small-businesspeople, yes.

MAYOR. Small businesses make up the majority of taxpayers here, the same as anywhere else.

ASLAKSEN. That's true enough.

MAYOR. And I've no doubt you know the general feeling amongst them. Isn't that so?

ASLAKSEN. Yes, I think I may safely say I do, Mr Mayor.

MAYOR. Well, the spirit of self-sacrifice being shown by our less affluent citizens is entirely praiseworthy, I must admit, but…

ASLAKSEN. What do you mean?

HOVSTAD. Self-sacrifice?

MAYOR. Yes, it's a superb manifestation of public-spiritedness – quite exceptional. I was on the point of saying unexpected, but you're obviously more in touch with these people than I am.

ASLAKSEN. Well, yes, Mr Mayor, but…

MAYOR. And in truth, it's no small sacrifice the town will be called upon to bear.

ASLAKSEN. The town?

HOVSTAD. The town?

ASLAKSEN. I don't understand. This is to do with the Baths, surely?

MAYOR. According to a preliminary estimate, the alterations which the Baths medical officer considers desirable will cost somewhere in the region of two hundred thousand crowns.

ASLAKSEN. That's a great deal of money, but…

MAYOR. Of course, it will be necessary to take out a municipal loan.

HOVSTAD (*stands up*). You're not suggesting that the town…

ASLAKSEN. You mean it's to come out of property taxes? Out of small-businesspeople's empty pockets?

MAYOR. My dear Mr Aslaksen, where else should the money come from?

ASLAKSEN. That's surely up to the gentlemen who own the Baths.

MAYOR. I'm afraid the proprietors aren't in a position to extend themselves any further.

ASLAKSEN. And are you quite certain of this, Mr Mayor?

MAYOR. Absolutely – I've made sure of it. If people really want these wholesale alterations, the town itself will have to pay for them.

ASLAKSEN. But damn it to hell – I beg your pardon! – but this is a different kettle of fish entirely, Mr Hovstad!

HOVSTAD. It most certainly is.

MAYOR. Of course, the worst part of all this is that we'll be forced to close the Baths for a good couple of years.

HOVSTAD. Close them! Completely?

ASLAKSEN. For two years!

MAYOR. Oh yes – that's how long the work will take – at least.

HOVSTAD. Yes, but ye gods! I mean, we'd never survive, Mr Mayor. What are people like us supposed to live on in the meantime?

MAYOR. Unfortunately, that's an extremely difficult question, Mr Aslaksen. But what do you expect us to do? I mean, do you imagine we'll have a single visitor to the Baths, if we go round spreading this delusion that the water here is polluted, that we're living in a plague spot, that the whole town...

ASLAKSEN. And it's all a delusion, is it?

MAYOR. With the best will in the world, I haven't been able to persuade myself otherwise.

ASLAKSEN. In that case, Dr Stockmann's behaviour is utterly inexcusable – I beg your pardon, Mr Mayor, but…

MAYOR. Unhappily, what you've just said is quite true, Mr Aslaksen. I'm afraid my brother's always been rather headstrong.

ASLAKSEN. Now, Mr Hovstad, are you still prepared to support him in this business?

HOVSTAD. Well, who would have believed…?

MAYOR. I've had a brief statement of the salient facts drawn up, as they might be interpreted by an impartial observer, and I've also included some suggestions as to how such deficiencies, as might in due course emerge, can reasonably be corrected within the limits of the Baths' own financial resources.

HOVSTAD. Do you have the statement with you, Mr Mayor?

MAYOR (*fumbling in his pocket*). Yes, I brought it with me on the off-chance you might…

ASLAKSEN (*hurriedly*). Oh God – that's him now!

MAYOR. Who? My brother?

HOVSTAD. Where? Where?

ASLAKSEN. He's coming through the press-room.

MAYOR. Damnation! I really don't want to bump into him here, and there's quite a lot I'd still like to discuss with you.

HOVSTAD (*pointing to the door at right*). You can wait in there meanwhile.

MAYOR. But…?

HOVSTAD. There's only Billing in there.

ASLAKSEN. Hurry, Mr Mayor – he's coming now.

MAYOR. Yes, all right – but try and get rid of him quickly.

He goes out through the door at right, as ASLAKSEN *opens it and closes it behind him.*

HOVSTAD. Look as if you're busy with something, Aslaksen.

He sits down and begins writing. ASLAKSEN *rummages through a pile of newspapers on a chair at right.*

DR STOCKMANN (*entering from the press-room*). Well, now – here I am again. (*Lays down his hat and stick.*)

HOVSTAD (*writing*). What, back already, doctor? You'll need to hurry up with that business we were talking about, Aslaksen. We've no time to spare today.

DR STOCKMANN (*to* ASLAKSEN). Proofs aren't ready yet, I gather.

ASLAKSEN (*without turning round*). No, doctor – no, I mean, you could hardly expect them.

DR STOCKMANN. No, of course not – it's just that I'm so impatient, as you can well imagine. I won't have a minute's peace until I've seen the article in print.

HOVSTAD. Hm… that'll be quite some time yet. Don't you think, Aslaksen?

ASLAKSEN. Yes, I'm afraid so.

DR STOCKMANN. That's fine, my dear friends. I'll come back. I'm happy to make two trips, if need be. With an issue of such importance – the welfare of the whole town – it's no time to be twiddling one's thumbs. (*About to go, but stops and returns.*) Oh, by the way – there's something else I wanted to discuss with you.

HOVSTAD. I'm sorry, doctor, but couldn't we leave it till another time…?

DR STOCKMANN. It won't take a minute. It's just this – you know, when people read my article in the paper tomorrow, and realise that I've spent the whole winter quietly working away for the good of the town…

HOVSTAD. Yes, doctor, but…

DR STOCKMANN. Now, I know what you're going to say. You'll say I was only damn well doing my duty – my simple duty as a citizen. Well, of course I was – I know that as well as you. But my fellow-citizens, you see… Well, dear God – these good people, they hold me in such high regard…

ASLAKSEN. Yes, indeed, the townsfolk have had the highest regard for you up till now, doctor.

DR STOCKMANN. Yes, and that's just what I'm afraid of… What I mean to say is… Well, when this reaches them – especially the less privileged classes – and they see it as a sort of incitement to take the running of the town's affairs into their own hands in future…

HOVSTAD (*rising*). Hm… Dr Stockmann, I don't want to keep this from you…

DR STOCKMANN. Aha! I knew there was something brewing! Well, I simply won't hear of it. So if they *are* planning anything of that kind…

HOVSTAD. Anything of what kind?

DR STOCKMANN. Oh, you know – whatever… a parade, or a banquet, or some sort of presentation, then I want you to promise faithfully that you'll nip it in the bud. You too, Mr Aslaksen, d'you hear?

HOVSTAD. Actually, doctor, we'd better tell you the truth, sooner rather than later...

MRS STOCKMANN, *in hat and coat, enters by the rear left door.*

MRS STOCKMANN (*catching sight of the* DOCTOR). Ah, I thought as much!

HOVSTAD (*going towards her*). You here too, Mrs Stockmann?

DR STOCKMANN. Katrine, what the devil are *you* doing here?

MRS STOCKMANN. You know perfectly well what I'm after.

HOVSTAD. Won't you have a seat? Or perhaps...

MRS STOCKMANN. Thanks, but don't worry about me. And you must excuse me coming here to fetch my husband. I'm the mother of three children, if you'd like to know.

DR STOCKMANN. Oh, for goodness' sake – we all know that.

MRS STOCKMANN. Well, it seems to me you think very little about your wife and children these days. Otherwise you wouldn't be doing this, driving us all to rack and ruin.

DR STOCKMANN. What, are you mad, Katrine? Just because a man has a wife and children, does that mean he's got no right to proclaim the truth? No right to be a useful, active citizen? No right to be of service to the town he lives in?

MRS STOCKMANN. Yes, but all things in moderation, Tomas!

ASLAKSEN. That's what I always say – everything in moderation.

MRS STOCKMANN. That's why you're doing us real harm, Mr Hovstad, luring my husband away from house and home, making a fool of him with all this business.

HOVSTAD. I'm not making a fool of anyone…

DR STOCKMANN. A fool? What, d'you think I'd let somebody make a fool out of *me*?

MRS STOCKMANN. Yes, that's exactly what you *would* do… Oh, I know, I know – you're the cleverest man in town, but you're so easily taken in, Tomas. (*To* HOVSTAD.) And just bear in mind that if you print that thing he's written, he'll lose his job at the Baths.

ASLAKSEN. What!

HOVSTAD. Well, yes, but you know, doctor…

DR STOCKMANN (*laughs*). Just let them try! No, no – they wouldn't dare. Because I've got that solid majority behind me, you see.

MRS STOCKMANN. Yes, that's the trouble – having a nasty thing like that at your back.

DR STOCKMANN. Oh, nonsense, Katrine. Now go home and look after the house – leave me to look after society. How can you be so frightened when I'm so confident and cheerful? (*Pacing up and down, rubbing his hands.*) Truth and the people will prevail, you can bet your life on it. Oh, I can see all the liberal-minded citizens coming together in one great victorious army…! (*Stops beside a chair.*) Good God, what the devil's this?

ASLAKSEN (*looking over*). Oh, dear!

HOVSTAD (*likewise*). Hm!

DR STOCKMANN. Well, well – here lies the very pinnacle of authority. (*Picks up the* MAYOR's *cap gingerly with his fingertips and holds it aloft.*)

MRS STOCKMANN. The Mayor's cap!

DR STOCKMANN. And his staff of office too. How in God's name… ?

HOVSTAD. Ah, well…

DR STOCKMANN. Oh, I see! He's been here trying to talk you round. Ha-ha! He'd come to the right place, hadn't he. And then he caught sight of me in the press-room… (*Bursts out laughing.*) So, has he run away, Mr Aslaksen?

ASLAKSEN (*hastily*). Oh yes, doctor – he's run away.

DR STOCKMANN. Run away without his cane or his… Oh, rubbish! Peter doesn't run away from anything. But where the devil have you hidden him? Oh, of course – in there! Now, just watch this, Katrine!

MRS STOCKMANN. Tomas – please!

ASLAKSEN. You'd better look out, doctor.

DR STOCKMANN *puts on the* MAYOR's *cap, picks up his cane and walks over to the door; he flings it open, and stands with his hand raised in salute. The* MAYOR *then emerges, red-faced with anger, and* BILLING *follows him in.*

MAYOR. What's all this carry-on about?

DR STOCKMANN. Let's have some respect, my dear Peter. Because I'm the authority here now. (*Paces up and down.*)

MRS STOCKMANN (*close to tears*). No, Tomas, don't!

MAYOR (*following him*). Give me my cap and stick!

DR STOCKMANN (*continuing*). You may be the chief of
police, but I'm the Mayor – I'm in charge of the whole
town, don't you see?

MAYOR. Take that cap off, I tell you. Just remember, that's
an official uniform cap!

DR STOCKMANN. Oh, tut-tut! D'you think the newly
awakened lion of the people is going to be scared of a
uniform cap? Yes, because you'd better know, we'll be
having a revolution in this town tomorrow. You threatened
to dismiss me, but now I'm dismissing you – relieving you
of all your official duties. What, you think I can't do it? Just
wait and see. Because I have the triumphant forces of
society on my side. Hovstad and Billing here will thunder
in *The People's Courier*, and Aslaksen will march out at the
head of the entire Homeowners' Association...

ASLAKSEN. I won't be doing that, doctor.

DR STOCKMANN. Of course you will.

MAYOR. Aha! Well, then, perhaps Mr Hovstad will end up
joining the rebels, eh?

HOVSTAD. No, Mr Mayor.

ASLAKSEN. No, Mr Hovstad isn't fool enough to ruin both
his paper and himself for the sake of some fanciful notion.

DR STOCKMANN (*looking around him*). What's all this about?

HOVSTAD. Actually, you presented your case in a false light,
doctor, and that's why I can't support it.

BILLING. No, and after what the Mayor was good enough to tell me in there…

DR STOCKMANN. A false light! Look, leave me to deal with that. You just print my article. I'm perfectly capable of defending it.

HOVSTAD. I'm not going to print it. I can't, and won't print it – I don't dare.

DR STOCKMANN. You don't dare? What sort of nonsense is that? You're the editor, aren't you? Surely it's the editors who control the press?

HOVSTAD. No, doctor, it's the readers.

MAYOR. Yes, it is, thank goodness.

ASLAKSEN. It's public opinion, the educated classes, homeowners and the like – it's *these* people who control the newspapers.

DR STOCKMANN (*comprehending*). And all these forces are ranged against me?

ASLAKSEN. Yes, doctor, they are. If your article were to be printed, it would mean absolute ruin for the town.

DR STOCKMANN. Really.

MAYOR. Now, my cap and stick!

DR STOCKMANN *takes off the cap and lays it on the table along with the* MAYOR's *cane. The* MAYOR *retrieves them.*

Well, that was an abrupt end to your term in office.

DR STOCKMANN. It's not ended yet. (*To* HOVSTAD.) So, it's quite impossible to get my article into the *Courier*?

HOVSTAD. Quite impossible. And I'm doing this out of respect for your family too, you know.

DR STOCKMANN. Oh? Well, you needn't concern yourself with my family, Mr Hovstad.

MAYOR (*takes a paper out of his pocket*). For public information purposes, it'll be sufficient to insert this. It's an official statement. Here you are.

HOVSTAD (*takes the paper*). Good – I'll make sure it goes in.

DR STOCKMANN. But not mine? You think you can silence me and suppress the truth! Well, you won't find it as easy as that. Mr Aslaksen, take my manuscript, please, and print it as a pamphlet immediately – at my own expense. I'd like four hundred copies – no, I'll take five, six hundred…

ASLAKSEN. No, doctor – even if you were to offer me its weight in gold, I wouldn't dream of lending my imprint to something like that. In the light of public opinion I wouldn't dare. You won't get that printed anywhere in town.

DR STOCKMANN. Well, give it back to me, then.

HOVSTAD (*hands him the manuscript*). Here you are.

DR STOCKMANN (*picks up his hat and stick*). It'll be made public, even so. I'll call a mass meeting and read it out. All my fellow-citizens are going to hear the voice of truth.

MAYOR. There isn't an organisation in town that'll let you hire a hall for that purpose.

ASLAKSEN. Not a single one – I'm positive about that.

BILLING. No, I'm damn sure they won't.

MRS STOCKMANN. Well, that would be utterly shameful.
But why is everyone turning against you now, Tomas?

DR STOCKMANN (*angrily*). I'll tell you why. It's because the
men in this town are nothing but a bunch of old women –
like you. All they care about is their families, and not about
the community.

MRS STOCKMANN (*taking his arm*). Then I'll show them
one… one old woman at least, who *can* be a man, for once
in her life. I'll stand by you, Tomas!

DR STOCKMANN. Well said, Katrine! And I'll speak out,
by God I will! If I can't rent a hall, then I'll hire a
drummer to march round the town with me, and read it
out at every street corner.

MAYOR. You're not going to act like a raving lunatic!

DR STOCKMANN. Indeed I am!

ASLAKSEN. You won't get a single man in the whole town to
go with you.

BILLING. I'm damn sure you won't!

MRS STOCKMANN. Don't give in, Tomas. I'll get the boys
to go with you.

DR STOCKMANN. That's an excellent idea!

MRS STOCKMANN. Morten'll be delighted to do it, and
Eilif'll go too.

DR STOCKMANN. And so will Petra! And yourself,
Katrine, of course!

MRS STOCKMANN. No no, not me. I'll stand by the
window and watch – that'll do me.

DR STOCKMANN (*flings his arms round her and kisses her*). Thank you! Now, gentlemen, let's test our mettle, shall we? Let's see if a pack of mean-spirited wretches have the power to gag a patriot who wants to clean up society!

STOCKMANN *and* KATRINE *go out through the door at rear left.*

MAYOR (*gravely shaking his head*). Now he's driven *her* crazy, too.

Curtain.

ACT FOUR

A large, old-fashioned room in CAPTAIN HORSTER's *house. Double doors at rear, standing open, lead to an anteroom. Along the wall at left are three windows; against the opposite wall a platform has been erected, with a small table, on which stand two candles, a carafe of water, a glass and a bell. The room is also illuminated by wall lamps placed between the windows. At left foreground stands a table with candles on it, and a chair; at right, another door, and a few chairs.*

A large crowd of TOWNSFOLK *of all classes is gathered, with several* WOMEN *and some* SCHOOLBOYS *among them. More and more people keep arriving through the door at rear, until the room is full.*

FIRST MAN (*bumping into another*). Lamstad! What, you here too?

SECOND MAN. Oh yes, I go to all the public meetings.

FIRST MAN. You'll have brought your whistle, then?

SECOND MAN. Wouldn't be without it. What about you?

THIRD MAN. I've got mine all right. And Skipper Evensen said he was going to bring his huge great cow-horn.

SECOND MAN. Good for Evensen!

They all laugh.

FOURTH MAN (*approaching*). Hey, listen – what's supposed to be happening here tonight?

SECOND MAN. It's Dr Stockmann. He's making a speech against the Mayor.

FOURTH MAN. Eh? But the Mayor's his brother.

FIRST MAN. So what? Dr Stockmann's not frightened of him.

THIRD MAN. Yes, but he's got it all wrong. At least, that's what it says in the *Courier.*

SECOND MAN. Yes, he obviously must be wrong this time, because nobody would rent him a hall – Homeowners' Association, Working Men's Clubs, nobody.

FIRST MAN. They wouldn't even let him have the hall at the Baths.

SECOND MAN. Well, that's no wonder.

A MAN (*in another group*). Whose side are we on in this business, would you say?

ANOTHER MAN (*in the same group*). Just watch Aslaksen, and do what *he* does.

BILLING (*with a portfolio under his arm, forcing his way through the crowd*). Excuse me, gentlemen! If you'll let me through, please? I'm reporting this for the *Courier.* Thank you very much! (*Sits down at the table, left.*)

A WORKMAN. So who's he?

SECOND WORKMAN. What, don't you know *him*? That's Billing – he works on Aslaksen's paper.

CAPTAIN HORSTER *leads* MRS STOCKMANN *and* PETRA *in through the door, downstage right.* EILIF *and* MORTEN *follow.*

HORSTER. I thought the family might sit here. Then if anything happened, you could slip out quietly.

MRS STOCKMANN. D'you think there'll be any trouble?

HORSTER. Well, you never know. With so many people here… Anyway, just sit down and take it easy.

MRS STOCKMANN (*sits down*). It was very good of you to offer Tomas the use of this room.

HORSTER. Well, when nobody else would…

PETRA (*who has also sat down*). And it was very brave of you, too, Captain Horster.

HORSTER. Oh, I don't think it took much courage.

HOVSTAD *and* ASLAKSEN *have arrived at the same time, but make their way forward through the crowd separately.*

ASLAKSEN (*going up to* HORSTER). Hasn't the doctor come yet?

HORSTER. He's waiting inside.

A movement in the crowd near the door at rear.

HOVSTAD (*to* BILLING). Here's the Mayor – look!

BILLING. Well, I'll be damned – he's turned up after all!

The MAYOR *steers his way slowly through the crowd, exchanging polite greetings, and positions himself by the wall, left. A moment later,* DR STOCKMANN *enters by the downstage right door. He is wearing a black frock coat and a white tie. A few people applaud hesitantly, to be met by subdued hissing. The room falls silent.*

DR STOCKMANN (*in an undertone*). How do you feel, Katrine?

MRS STOCKMANN. I'm fine, thanks. (*Lowers her voice.*) Now, try not to lose your temper, Tomas.

DR STOCKMANN. Oh, don't worry – I can control myself. (*Looks at his watch, steps up onto the platform, and bows.*) Well, it's quarter past now, so I'd like to begin… (*Takes his manuscript out of his pocket.*)

ASLAKSEN. We really ought to appoint a chairman first.

DR STOCKMANN. No, that's hardly necessary.

SEVERAL VOICES (*shouting*). Yes! Yes!

MAYOR. Yes, I think I'd like to see some sort of chairman elected, too.

DR STOCKMANN. Peter, I've only called this meeting to present my paper.

MAYOR. Yes, but the chief medical officer's paper might well lead to some conflict of opinion.

MORE VOICES (*from the crowd*). A chairman! A chairman!

HOVSTAD. Well, the general consensus seems to be in favour of a chairman.

DR STOCKMANN (*restraining himself*). All right – let's bow to the will of the people, then.

ASLAKSEN. Wouldn't the Mayor himself like to take on that role?

THREE MEN (*applauding*). Bravo! Bravo!

MAYOR. No, for a variety of reasons, which are obvious enough, I think, I must decline. However, fortunately we have in our midst a man whom I believe we can all accept. I'm referring, of course, to the chairman of the Homeowners' Association – Mr Aslaksen.

MANY VOICES. Yes, yes! Aslaksen! Hurrah for Aslaksen!

DR STOCKMANN *picks up his manuscript and paces up and down the platform.*

ASLAKSEN. Well, if my fellow citizens choose to put their trust in me, I can hardly refuse…

Clapping and shouts of approval. ASLAKSEN *mounts the platform.*

BILLING (*writing*). Now, then… 'Mr Aslaksen's election unanimously approved…'

ASLAKSEN. And since I now find myself in this situation, I should like to say a few brief words, if I may. I am a quiet, peace-loving man, who believes in discreet moderation… and moderate discretion. Anyone who knows me will bear witness to that.

MANY VOICES. Yes! That's right, Aslaksen!

ASLAKSEN. From long experience in the school of life, I've learned that moderation is the most precious virtue a citizen can possess…

MAYOR. Hear, hear!

ASLAKSEN. And furthermore, that discretion and moderation are what best serve society. That's why I would urge the distinguished fellow-citizen who has called this meeting to make every effort to remain within the bounds of moderation.

A DRUNK MAN (*by the door*). Three cheers for the Temperance Union!

A VOICE. Shame on you!

MANY VOICES. Ssshh! Ssshh!

ASLAKSEN. Gentlemen, please – no interruptions! Now, does anyone have anything to add?

MAYOR. Mr Chairman!

ASLAKSEN. Yes, Mr Mayor…

MAYOR. Sir, in view of the close relationship which, as is well known, exists between myself and the medical officer presently employed at the Baths, I should have preferred not to speak this evening. However, my official connection with the Baths, not to mention my solicitude for the town's vital interests, compel me to bring forward a motion. I think I may safely say that not a single one of us citizens, assembled here today, would wish to see irresponsible and exaggerated accounts of sanitary conditions at the Baths, and the town in general, made public and circulated abroad.

MANY VOICES. No! No! Never! We protest!

MAYOR. I therefore move that this meeting refuse permission for the medical officer to read, or otherwise comment on his report.

DR STOCKMANN (*flaring up*). Refuse permission! What's this?

MRS STOCKMANN (*coughs*). Ahem!

DR STOCKMANN (*controlling himself*). Refuse permission, eh? Well, well…

MAYOR. In my official statement to *The People's Courier*, I've already acquainted the public with the relevant facts, so that any fair-minded person can perfectly well form his own opinion. You'll see there that the doctor's proposal – apart from being in effect a vote of no confidence in the town's leadership – would actually burden local ratepayers with an unnecessary expenditure of at least a hundred thousand crowns.

Shouts of outrage, and whistling.

ASLAKSEN (*ringing his bell*). Order, gentlemen, please! Now, I'd like to second the Mayor's motion. I'm also of the opinion that all this fuss the doctor is making conceals an ulterior motive. He talks about the Baths, but what he's really after is revolution. He'd like to see the running of this town taken over by other hands. Nobody doubts the doctor's honourable intentions – goodness, no, on that point, there is absolutely no question. For that matter, I'm also in favour of self-government, as long as it doesn't hit the ratepayer too hard. In the present case, however, that's exactly what would happen. And that's why… if you'll forgive me, gentlemen – that's why I'm damned if I can support Dr Stockmann on this occasion. You can pay too high a price, even for gold – that's *my* opinion.

Vigorous approval on all sides.

HOVSTAD. I feel duty bound to clarify my position also. Dr Stockmann's campaign seemed to be attracting a good deal of support in its early days and I gave it my backing, as impartially as I could. But eventually it dawned on us that we had allowed ourselves to be misled by a false interpretation…

DR STOCKMANN. False!

HOVSTAD. Well, not wholly reliable, let's say. The Mayor's statement made that clear. I hope no one here has any doubts as to my liberal sentiments – the position adopted by *The People's Courier* on the important political questions of our time is well known. But I have learned, from men of wisdom and experience, that in dealing with purely local issues, a newspaper must proceed with a certain caution.

ASLAKSEN. I'm in complete agreement with the speaker.

HOVSTAD. And in the matter now before us, it is beyond dispute that Dr Stockmann has the weight of public opinion against him. But first and foremost, gentlemen, what is the prime duty of an editor? Isn't it to work in harmony with his readers? Doesn't he have a sort of unspoken mandate to labour diligently and unceasingly for the well-being of those whose views he represents? Or is it possible I'm simply mistaken?

MANY VOICES. No! No! Hovstad's right!

HOVSTAD. It's been a painful struggle for me to break with a man in whose home I've lately been a frequent guest; a man who, until today, could rejoice in the undivided goodwill of his fellow-citizens; a man whose only fault... or at least his greatest fault, is that he follows his heart, rather than his head.

SOME SCATTERED VOICES. That's true! Hurrah for Dr Stockmann!

HOVSTAD. But my duty to the community obliged me to break with him. And there's another consideration which prompts me to oppose him, and if possible, to prevent him going any further along this fateful path he has chosen; that is, consideration for his family...

DR STOCKMANN. Stick to the water supply and the sewers!

HOVSTAD. ... Consideration for his wife, and his neglected children.

MORTEN. Does he mean us, Mother?

MRS STOCKMANN. Ssh!

ASLAKSEN. So, I shall now put the Mayor's proposal to a vote.

DR STOCKMANN. Don't even bother! I've no intention of speaking about that filthy mess at the Baths tonight. No, you're going to hear something quite different.

MAYOR (*in an undertone*). What's he up to now?

A DRUNK MAN (*by the door*). I pay rates, so I've got rights! I've got the right to an opinion! And I'm fully... I'm firmly... I'm in comp... in comp... incomprehensible...

SEVERAL VOICES. Be quiet over there!

OTHERS. He's drunk! Throw him out!

The DRUNK MAN *is put outside.*

DR STOCKMANN. Now – may I speak?

ASLAKSEN (*rings the bell*). Dr Stockmann has the floor!

DR STOCKMANN. Just a few days ago, I'd like to have seen anyone dare to try and silence me, as they have done here tonight. I'd have defended my sacred human rights like a lion! Now, I no longer care, because I have something to say to you of far greater importance.

The CROWD *press closer to him.* MORTEN KIIL *is conspicuous among them.*

(*Continuing.*) I've been doing a lot of thinking these past few days – pondering a whole range of things till in the end it seemed as if my head was spinning...

MAYOR (*coughs*). Ahem!

DR STOCKMANN. But I finally got everything clear in my mind, and I could see the truth, which is why I'm standing here before you tonight. Yes, I have a great revelation to make to you, my fellow-citizens! For I have made a truly important discovery – far greater than the trivial matter of our water supply being poisoned, or the fact that our municipal Baths are sited over a cesspit…

MANY VOICES (*shouting*). Don't talk about the Baths! We don't want to hear it! That's enough of that!

DR STOCKMANN. I have said I would talk about the great discovery I have made over the past few days – the discovery that all the sources of our *spiritual* life are polluted, and that the entire fabric of our society is built on a plague-ridden foundation of lies.

DISCONCERTED VOICES (*muttering*). What's he saying?

MAYOR. Really, that sort of insinuation…

ASLAKSEN (*with his hand on the bell*). The speaker will kindly moderate his language.

DR STOCKMANN. For many years now I have loved my hometown as much as any man can, that place where he spent the days of his youth. Nor was I very old when I left here, and distance, the feeling of exile, all my fond memories, have cast something akin to an enchanted glow over both this town, and its people.

Sporadic applause and cheering.

Anyway, later, I spent a number of years in a wretched, godforsaken hole in the far north. And every time I encountered one of those poor, starving creatures who lived up there, scattered amongst their barren rocks, I would think how much more useful it would've been, had they been sent a vet, instead of a man such as myself.

Some murmuring in the room.

BILLING (*putting his pen down*) Well, I'll be damned – I've never heard the like!

HOVSTAD. That's a slander on perfectly respectable folk!

DR STOCKMANN. Now, just hold on a minute! I trust nobody would dare to suggest that I forgot my own hometown up there. No, I brooded over it night and day, the way an eider duck does with her egg. And my great project was duly hatched – the establishment of our municipal Baths.

Mixed applause and protests.

And when Fate finally decreed that I should experience the joy of coming home again – yes, my friends, at that time I believed I had nothing left to wish for – but no, I had one more desire on this earth: a sincere, insistent, burning desire to work for the benefit of my hometown, and of its people.

MAYOR (*staring into space*). You have a strange way of… Ahem!

DR STOCKMANN. And so I went around town, blind to everything but my happiness. However, since yesterday morning – no, actually the night before – I've had my eyes wide open, and the first thing I've noticed is the sheer, unbounded stupidity of the authorities…

Various noises, shouts and laughter. MRS STOCKMANN *coughs insistently.*

MAYOR. Mr Chairman!

ASLAKSEN (*ringing his bell*). By the power vested in me…!

DR STOCKMANN. Oh, that's ridiculous, Mr Aslaksen –
picking me up on a word. All I meant was that I've come to
realise just what an unholy mess our leading lights are
responsible for, down there at the Baths. Frankly, I can't
abide these so-called leaders of men – and God knows, I've
seen enough of them in my day. They're like goats in a
stand of young trees – they wreak havoc wherever they go.
They get in a free man's way, no matter what he tries to do,
and I'd love to see them all exterminated, like any other
noxious creature…

Uproar.

MAYOR. Mr Chairman! Are you going to allow such
expressions to pass?

ASLAKSEN (*with his hand on the bell*). Dr Stockmann!

DR STOCKMANN. I can't understand why it's taken me so
long to waken up to the true nature of these gentlemen,
when I've had a perfect example of the breed, staring me
in the face, almost every day – I mean my brother Peter –
slow on the uptake, and set in his ways…

Laughter, general commotion and whistling. MRS
STOCKMANN *sits coughing.* ASLAKSEN *violently rings his
bell.*

DRUNK MAN (*who has come back in*). Are you talking about
me? All right, so my name *is* Pettersen, but I'll be damned
if I…

ANGRY VOICES. Get that drunk out of here! Throw him
out!

The DRUNK MAN *is again ejected.*

MAYOR. Who was that person?

A BYSTANDER. I've no idea who he is, Mr Mayor.

ANOTHER. He isn't from this town.

A THIRD. I think he's a timber merchant, sir – comes from…
   (*The remainder is inaudible.*)

ASLAKSEN. The man's obviously had too much beer. Carry
   on, Dr Stockmann, but please, try to exercise a little
   moderation.

DR STOCKMANN. Very well, sirs – I shall say no more on
   the subject of our leaders. After what I've just said, though,
   if anyone should imagine that I set out with the express
   aim of attacking these gentlemen this evening, they'd be
   wrong – wholly and utterly mistaken. In fact, I hold to the
   comforting conviction that all these old fogeys, these relics
   of a bygone age, are doing a first-rate job in bringing on
   their own demise – they don't need any doctor's help to
   speed up the process. Besides which, it isn't those sort of
   people who constitute the greatest threat to society; it isn't
   they who are most actively engaged in poisoning the
   sources of our spiritual life, and polluting the very ground
   beneath us; it isn't they who are the most dangerous
   enemies to truth and freedom in our society.

SHOUTS FROM ALL SIDES. Who are, then? Who are
   they? Name them!

DR STOCKMANN. Oh, I'll name them, have no fear of
   that. Because that's precisely the great discovery I made
   yesterday. (*Raising his voice.*) The most dangerous enemies to
   truth and freedom in our midst – are the so-called solid
   majority. Yes, indeed – that damned solid liberal majority,
   that's who they are. So now you know.

Uproar in the room – most people are shouting, stamping their feet, and whistling. Some of the OLDER MEN *in the crowd exchange furtive glances, and seem to be enjoying themselves.* MRS STOCKMANN *stands up anxiously.* EILIF *and* MORTEN *advance menacingly on some* SCHOOLBOYS, *who are misbehaving.* ASLAKSEN *rings his bell, calling the meeting to order.* HOVSTAD *and* BILLING *are having a conversation, but inaudible. Finally, peace is restored.*

ASLAKSEN. As chairman, I call upon the speaker to withdraw his tactless remarks.

DR STOCKMANN. Never, Mr Aslaksen – absolutely not. That is the very same majority in our community, which is trying to rob me of my freedom, and prevent me from speaking the truth.

HOVSTAD. The majority always has right on its side.

BILLING. And the truth too, God damn it!

DR STOCKMANN. The majority never has right on its side. Never, I say! That's one of those social lies that a free, thinking individual has to rebel against. Just who make up the majority in any country? Is it the intelligent people, or the idiots? I think we may safely say that the idiots are in a quite alarmingly overwhelming majority these days, the whole world over. But for heaven's sake, that surely doesn't mean that the idiotic should have power over the intelligent?

Uproar, shouting.

Oh, yes, you can shout me down, but you can't contradict me. The majority has *might* on its side, unfortunately – but *right* it has not. Whereas I, along with a very few other people, *do* have right. The minority is always in the right.

Renewed uproar.

HOVSTAD (*laughs*). So, in the past couple of days, Dr Stockmann has joined the aristocracy?

DR STOCKMANN. I've already said I wasn't going to waste my breath on that pack of narrow-chested, weak-kneed creatures puffing and panting along behind us. The raw, pulsating life of action no longer concerns them. No, I'm thinking of those few amongst us, who have managed to absorb all the fresh new ideas that have been germinating. These men are like an advance guard at a frontier post, so far ahead that the 'solid majority' hasn't yet caught up with them. And there they stand, bravely fighting for truths, too newly born into the world of consciousness to have any sort of majority to defend them.

HOVSTAD. So the doctor's become a revolutionary now?

DR STOCKMANN. Yes, by God, I have, Mr Hovstad! I'm launching a revolution against the false principle that the majority have some kind of monopoly on the truth. And what exactly are these truths which the majority set such store by? Why, they're truths so ancient that they're positively decrepit. And when a truth gets to that stage, you might as well call it a lie, gentlemen, since that's where it's headed anyway.

Laughter and jeering.

Yes, yes, you can believe it if you like. But truths aren't at all the tough old Methuselahs people imagine. An ordinary established truth lives for… oh, let's say seventeen or eighteen years as a rule, twenty at most, seldom any longer. However, these old truths, always so frightfully meagre, are the only thing that concerns the majority, and the only thing they're prepared to offer society, by way of food for the soul. But there's precious little nourishment to be found in that sort of food, I assure you, and as a doctor I know what I'm talking about. All these majority truths are like last year's cured meat gone bad – like putrid, tainted ham. And that's the root cause of all the moral scurvy that's now rampant in our communities.

ASLAKSEN. It seems to me that the honourable speaker is straying some way from his subject.

MAYOR. I'm afraid I must agree with the chairman there.

DR STOCKMANN. Well, I think you must be mad, Peter. I'm sticking as closely as I can to the subject at issue, since that's just what I'm talking about: the mass of the people, that selfsame majority – that damned solid majority. That's what's poisoning all the sources of our moral life, and polluting the very soil under our feet.

HOVSTAD. And the great liberal majority, you say, are doing all this because they have the good sense to restrict their approval to well-founded and widely accepted truths?

DR STOCKMANN. My dear Mr Hovstad, please don't talk to me about well-founded truths. These truths of yours, which the masses are prepared to accept, are the ones judged to be well-founded by progressive thinkers in our grandfathers' day. However, those of us who man the frontier posts nowadays can no longer accept them, and in my view the only incontrovertible truth is this: that no society can live a healthy life, feeding on the old dry bones of that kind of truth.

HOVSTAD. Yes, well, instead of standing there letting off steam, it would be more interesting if you actually specified what these old dry bones are, that we're supposed to be feeding on.

Signs of approval from various quarters.

DR STOCKMANN. Oh, I could draw up a long list of horrors, but for the moment I'll stick to one widely accepted truth, which is basically a monstrous lie, but which nonetheless has the support not only of Mr Hovstad, and *The People's Courier*, but all their loyal subscribers.

HOVSTAD. And that is…?

DR STOCKMANN. That is the doctrine you've inherited from your forefathers, and which is promulgated far and wide throughout the land – the doctrine which claims that the working classes, the great unwashed, are in fact the cream of the nation, the *populus*, the very essence of the people, and that these, the most immature and ignorant individuals in society, have the same right to judge, to approve, to direct and to govern, as the few rare beings of genuine intellectual accomplishment.

BILLING. Well, I'll be damned…!

HOVSTAD (*simultaneously, shouting*). You hear that, citizens? Write that down!

SEVERAL VOICES. Ho-ho! So we aren't the people? Only the aristocrats have rights, is that it?

A WORKER. Fling him out, he shouldn't say things like that.

OTHERS. Out with him! Throw him out the door!

A MAN (*shouts*). Evensen, blow your horn!

Loud blasts on the horn, whistling, the room in uproar.

DR STOCKMANN (*after the noise has subsided slightly*). Look, be reasonable. Can't you stand to hear the truth for once? I didn't expect you all to agree with me this instant, but I did hope that Mr Hovstad might admit I was right, when he'd calmed down a bit. I mean, Mr Hovstad claims to be a freethinker...

SHOCKED VOICES. Freethinker, did he say? Who is? Is Hovstad a freethinker?

HOVSTAD (*shouts*). Prove it, Dr Stockmann. When have I ever said that in print?

DR STOCKMANN (*after some thought*). No, damn it, you're absolutely right. You've never had the guts. Well, I don't want to make trouble for you, Mr Hovstad, so let's just say that I'm the only freethinker here. Because now I'm going to prove to you scientifically, that when the *Courier* tells you that you, the general public, the so-called shadowy masses, are the very essence of the people – then that same *Courier* is leading you most shamefully by the nose. That's just a journalist's lie, that's all. The general public are nothing more than the raw material out of which a true *populus* is made.

Mutterings, laughter, sounds of unrest in the room.

But isn't that just a fact of life? Isn't there a vast difference between a pedigree animal and a crossbreed? Look at a common barnyard hen, for instance. What sort of food value would you expect from a scrawny, leathery old specimen like that? Not much, I'd wager. And what kind of eggs would it lay? Any self-respecting crow or raven can lay every bit as good an egg. But you take a purebred Spanish or Japanese hen, or a decent pheasant or turkey, even – and you'll soon see the difference. Or again, look at dogs – creatures we humans resemble in so many ways. First, think of an ordinary stray dog – I mean one of those nasty, ill-bred, scruffy little tykes that run round the streets, relieving themselves at every corner. Then compare one of these mongrels with a poodle whose pedigree goes back several generations, in a gentleman's house where he's been well fed, and grown up listening to soft, harmonious voices, and good music. Don't you think the poodle's brain will have developed quite differently from the mongrel's? Of course it will! Poodles like that have pups, and showmen can train them up to do all sorts of fantastic tricks that your ordinary mongrel could never manage, not even if you stood him on his head.

Uproar and general mockery.

A CITIZEN (*shouts*). What, are you trying to turn us all into dogs now?

ANOTHER MAN. We're not animals, doctor!

DR STOCKMANN. Oh, but we *are* animals, my friend! And by and large, we're as good animals as any man could wish for. But even amongst us, you won't find too many outstanding specimens. Yes, indeed, there's a world of difference between poodles and mongrels of the human variety. And what's very funny, really, is that Mr Hovstad wholeheartedly agrees with me, as long as it's only four-legged animals we're discussing…

HOVSTAD. Yes, well, it's true enough for *them*!

DR STOCKMANN. Exactly. But the minute I extend that principle to bipeds, Mr Hovstad stops in his tracks. He no longer dares to think his own thoughts, or to pursue them to their logical conclusion. So he turns the whole idea upside down, and declares in *The People's Courier* that barnyard hens and street tykes are the finest specimens in the entire menagerie. But that's always the way, isn't it, when a man remains stuck in a mental rut, and hasn't managed to arrive at some kind of intellectual distinction.

HOVSTAD. I make no claim to any kind of distinction. I come from simple peasant stock, and I'm proud that my roots lie among those same common people he insults.

SEVERAL WORKMEN. Good for you, Hovstad! You tell him!

DR STOCKMANN. No, the sort of common people I'm talking about aren't just at the bottom of the social heap, they're buzzing and swarming all around us, right up to the very highest ranks of society. You've only got to look at our fine, upstanding Mayor! My brother Peter is as common as any man that ever wore shoes…

Laughter and hissing.

MAYOR. I object most strongly to these personal allusions.

DR STOCKMANN (*unperturbed*) And it's nothing to do with the fact that he's descended from some old Pomeranian pirate – we are, actually.

MAYOR. Ridiculous – an old wives' tale!

DR STOCKMANN. No, it's because he thinks only what his superiors think, and believes what they believe. Well, people who do that are as common as muck, intellectually speaking, which is why my illustrious brother Peter is so lacking in natural distinction – and as a consequence, so narrow-minded.

MAYOR. Mr Chairman…!

HOVSTAD. So the only men of distinction in this country are the freethinkers? No, there's a turn-up for the book!

Laughter.

DR STOCKMANN. Yes, that's something else I've
discovered. And along with it goes the conviction that
freethinking is practically the same as morality. That's why
I say it's downright inexcusable of the *Courier* to carry on,
day in day out, proclaiming the heresy that the common
people, the so-called 'solid majority', occupy some sort of
moral high ground, while every vice, every manifestation of
corruption and depravity, is somehow filtered down from
culture, just as all the disgusting filth in our Baths is filtered
down from the tanneries up at Mølledal!

Uproar and shouts of protest.

(*Carries on regardless, impassioned, smiling.*) Yet this selfsame
People's Courier thunders on about raising the masses onto a
higher plane of existence! Good God, if the *Courier*'s got it
right, then elevating the masses would be tantamount to
whipping them straight down the primrose path to
perdition! Fortunately, the notion that culture is a corrupting
influence is another old wives' tale. No, it's stupidity, poverty,
the sheer ugliness of life, that do the devil's work! In a house
that isn't swept clean and aired every day – my wife Katrine
maintains the floor should be scrubbed as well, but that's a
moot point… Anyway, a person forced to live two or three
years in such a house, I would say, will tend to lose all sense
of morality. Lack of oxygen causes the conscience to
suffocate. And there's no shortage of houses lacking oxygen,
many of them in this town, it would appear, if the 'solid
majority' is so devoid of conscience as to seek to build its
prosperity on a morass of lies and deceit.

ASLAKSEN. Making serious allegations like that against the
whole community – that's outrageous!

A GENTLEMAN. I call on the chairman to rule the speaker out of order!

ANGRY VOICES. Yes! Yes! That's right – rule him out of order!

DR STOCKMANN (*flaring up*). Then I'll proclaim the truth from every street corner! I'll write to the press! I'll make sure the whole country knows what's going on here!

HOVSTAD. It seems Dr Stockmann's hell-bent on ruining this town.

DR STOCKMANN. That's right – I love my hometown so much that I'd rather destroy it than see it prosper on a lie.

ASLAKSEN. Those are strong words, doctor.

Shouting and whistling. MRS STOCKMANN *coughs loudly in vain.* DR STOCKMANN *no longer hears her.*

HOVSTAD (*through the uproar*). Any man who would destroy a whole community must be an enemy of the people!

DR STOCKMANN (*as the hissing grows louder*). When that whole community is shot through with lies, it *should* be destroyed! Raze it to the ground, I say. Get rid of it. People who live by lies should be exterminated, like vermin! Pretty soon you'll have the whole country infested, and it too will deserve to be destroyed! If that day should ever come, then I tell you, from the very bottom of my heart, I'd happily see the whole country laid waste, the entire nation wiped out!

A MAN (*among the crowd*). Spoken like a true enemy of the people!

BILLING. And that, God damn it, is the *voice* of the people!

CROWD (*shouting*). Yes, yes, yes! He's an enemy of the people! He hates his own country! He hates his own nation!

ASLAKSEN. Well, I'm speaking now as a Norwegian citizen, *and* a private person, and let me tell you I'm deeply disturbed at what I've had to listen to. Dr Stockmann has shown himself up in a manner I should never have dreamt possible. I regret to say, therefore, that I wholeheartedly concur with the views just expressed by my distinguished fellow-citizens. And I move that we give that opinion due weight in a formal resolution. I propose the following: 'This assembly formally declares Dr Tomas Stockmann, superintendent of the Municipal Baths, to be an enemy of the people.'

Loud cheers and applause. Some of the crowd confront DR STOCKMANN, *jeering and catcalling.* MRS STOCKMANN *and* PETRA *get to their feet, while* MORTEN *and* EILIF *fight with the other* SCHOOLBOYS, *who have joined in the catcalling, until the grown-ups separate them.*

DR STOCKMANN (*to the baying mob*). You fools, you blind fools! I tell you…

ASLAKSEN (*ringing his bell*). Dr Stockmann, you no longer have the floor. A formal vote now has to take place, but to save embarrassment and preserve anonymity, I propose that we record it on a blank piece of paper, unsigned. Mr Billing, do you have any blank paper?

BILLING. I've got both blue and white.

ASLAKSEN (*steps down*). That's excellent – it'll be quicker that way. Cut the sheets into little pieces. Yes, yes – like that. (*To the meeting*) Now, blue stands for a 'No' vote, white stands for a 'Yes'. I'll come round and collect the votes myself.

The MAYOR *goes out of the room, while* ASLAKSEN *and a couple of other* CITIZENS *collect the votes in their hats.*

A MAN (*to* HOVSTAD). What on earth's happened to the doctor? Eh? What do you make of all this?

HOVSTAD. Well, you know how headstrong he is.

ANOTHER MAN (*to* BILLING). Tell me – you're quite often in his house – has he taken to drink, have you noticed?

BILLING. I don't know what to say, God damn it, but there's always hot toddy brought out when anybody calls.

A THIRD MAN. No, I think he's gone off his rocker.

FIRST MAN. Isn't there some history of insanity in the family?

BILLING. I don't know – it's quite possible.

A FOURTH MAN. No, it's pure spite, that's all. He's getting his own back on somebody for some insult or other.

BILLING. Actually, he did say something once about an increase in his retainer, but he didn't get it.

ALL THE MEN (*together*). Ah well, there's your answer.

DRUNK MAN (*in the crowd*). I want a blue one! And I want a white one as well!

SHOUTS. It's that drunk again – throw him out!

MORTEN KIIL (*goes over to the* DOCTOR). Well, Stockmann, you see where your monkey tricks have landed you?

DR STOCKMANN. I've done my duty, that's all.

MORTEN KIIL. What was that you said about the tanneries up at Mølledal?

DR STOCKMANN. You heard me. I said that was where all the filth was coming from.

MORTEN KIIL. From my tannery too?

DR STOCKMANN. Unfortunately, your tannery's the worst of the lot.

MORTEN KIIL. And you going to put that in the newspaper?

DR STOCKMANN. I'm holding nothing back.

MORTEN KIIL. That might cost you dear, Stockmann. (*Goes out.*)

FAT MAN (*goes over to* CAPTAIN HORSTER, *without acknowledging the* LADIES). So, Captain, you rent your rooms out to enemies of the people?

HORSTER. I think I can do what I like with my own property, Mr Vik.

FAT MAN. So you'll have no objection if I do the same with mine?

HORSTER. Meaning what?

FAT MAN. You'll find out tomorrow. (*Turns round and goes out.*)

PETRA. Wasn't that your shipowner, Captain Horster?

HORSTER. Yes, that was Mr Vik, the wholesaler.

ASLAKSEN (*holding the voting slips in his hand, steps up onto the platform and rings his bell*). Gentlemen, let me announce the result. With one exception, all the votes…

YOUNG MAN. That was that drunk.

ASLAKSEN. With the exception of one drunk person, the resolution is carried unanimously, to the effect that the superintendent of the Baths, Dr Tomas Stockmann, is hereby declared an enemy of the people.

Shouting and applause.

Long live our ancient and honourable community!

Applause.

Three cheers for our capable and efficient Mayor, for so loyally suppressing family ties!

Applause.

The meeting is now adjourned. (*Steps down from the platform.*)

BILLING. A vote of thanks to the chair!

WHOLE CROWD. Three cheers for Mr Aslaksen, the printer!

DR STOCKMANN. Petra, my hat and coat, please. Captain Horster, have you room for any passengers on board, to the New World?

HORSTER. For you and yours, doctor, I can certainly make room.

DR STOCKMANN (*while* PETRA *helps him on with his coat*). Good. Come along, Katrine. Come along, boys. (*Takes his wife by the arm.*)

MRS STOCKMANN (*quietly*). Tomas dear, let's go out by the back door.

DR STOCKMANN. No no – no back door for us, Katrine. (*Raising his voice.*) You'll hear more from this enemy of the people, before he quits this town for good. I'm not as gentle as a certain person, well known to you. No, I'm not saying I forgive you, for you know not what you do!

ASLAKSEN (*shouts*). Dr Stockmann, that comparison is blasphemous!

BILLING. God damn it, so it is – what a terrible thing to say in front of respectable people!

A HOARSE VOICE. And the threats he was making!

ANGRY SHOUTS. Let's break his windows! Duck him in the fjord!

A MAN IN THE CROWD. Give him a blast on your horn, Evensen! Toot-toot!

Horn blasts, whistling, wild shouting. The DOCTOR *and his family make their way out,* HORSTER *clearing a path for them.*

THE WHOLE CROWD (*howling after them*). Enemy of the people! Enemy of the people!

BILLING (*gathering up his papers*). Well, I'm damned if I'd fancy drinking toddy at Stockmann's place tonight!

The assembled crowd disperse. Shouts continue to be heard from outside in the street. 'Enemy of the people! Enemy of the people!'

Curtain.

ACT FIVE

DR STOCKMANN's *study. Bookcases and an assortment of medicine cabinets line the walls. In the rear wall, a door leading out to the hallway. Downstage left, a door to the living room. In the wall at right, two windows, the panes of which have been smashed. In the centre of the room is the* DOCTOR's *writing table, covered with books and papers. The room is an untidy mess. It is morning.*

DR STOCKMANN, *in his dressing gown and slippers and wearing a skullcap, is crouched on the floor, poking with an umbrella under one of the cabinets. Finally, he manages to rake out a stone.*

DR STOCKMANN (*calling through the open living-room door*). That's another one, Katrine.

MRS STOCKMANN (*from the living room*). And you'll find plenty more, I've no doubt.

DR STOCKMANN (*adds the stone to a pile already on the table*). I'm going to keep these stones as a memorial, a sort of holy relic. Eilif and Morten will see them every day, and when they grow up they'll inherit them. (*Raking under another bookcase.*) That girl – what's her name, damn it – has she gone for the glazier yet?

MRS STOCKMANN (*entering*). Yes, she has, but he wasn't sure if he could come today.

DR STOCKMANN. No, he doesn't dare – you wait and see.

MRS STOCKMANN. That's what Randine thought too – he'd be afraid of the neighbours. (*Calling into the living room.*)

Yes, Randine, what do you want? Oh, I see. (*Goes in and comes back immediately.*) It's a letter for you, Tomas.

DR STOCKMANN. Let me see. (*Opens it and reads.*) Hah!

MRS STOCKMANN. Who is it from?

DR STOCKMANN. It's from the landlord. He's giving us notice to quit.

MRS STOCKMANN. Honestly? He seemed such a nice man.

DR STOCKMANN (*looking again at the letter*). He's very sorry, he says, but he daren't do otherwise... because of his fellow-citizens... in deference to public opinion... not independent... daren't risk upsetting influential people...

MRS STOCKMANN. There, you see, Tomas?

DR STOCKMANN. Yes, yes, I see all right – they're all cowards, they're all the same in this town. Nobody dares do anything, for fear of other people. (*Flings the letter down on the table.*) But that doesn't matter to us, Katrine. We're headed for the New World now, so...

MRS STOCKMANN. Yes, Tomas, but have we really thought this through – this business of leaving?

DR STOCKMANN. How can I possibly stay here, where they've held me up to ridicule as a public enemy, branded me a criminal, smashed my windows? And look, Katrine, see – they've torn a hole in my trousers!

MRS STOCKMANN. Oh, no! And they're your best ones, too!

DR STOCKMANN. You should never wear your best trousers when you're fighting for truth and freedom. Well, I'm not too bothered about the trousers – you can always

stitch them up for me. But the fact that that rabble out
there are going after me as if they were my equals – damn
it, that makes my blood boil!

MRS STOCKMANN. Yes, they've been really nasty to you in
this town, Tomas, but does that mean we have to leave the
country altogether?

DR STOCKMANN. Don't you think you'll find the same
mindless rabble in other towns, as well as this one? They're
all the same. No, to hell with them, let them say what they
like. That's not the worst thing – no, it's the fact that all over
this country people adhere slavishly to the party line. As for
that, it's unlikely to be much better in the free west either.
It'll be just the same there, the same solid majorities, the
same 'liberal' public opinion, and all that other nonsense.
But everything's on a bigger scale there, you see. They might
kill you, but they won't torture you, they won't put your soul
on the rack. And if necessary, you can keep yourself to
yourself. (*Pacing the floor.*) I only wish I knew of a primeval
forest somewhere, or a South Sea Island, going cheap…

MRS STOCKMANN. But what about the boys, Tomas?

DR STOCKMANN (*comes to a halt*). You're joking, Katrine,
surely? Would you rather the boys grew up in a society like
ours? You saw for yourself last night that half the
population is stark raving mad, and if the other half
haven't lost their wits entirely, it's because they had none to
lose.

MRS STOCKMANN. Tomas dear, you really need to be
more careful what you say.

DR STOCKMANN. Well? Isn't it true, what I'm saying?
Don't they turn every sensible idea upside down? Don't
they make an utter shambles of everything, confusing right

and wrong? Don't they take lies and call them truth? Have
you ever heard the like, Katrine? It's all very silly, I know,
but…

PETRA *enters from the living room.*

MRS STOCKMANN. Back from school already?

PETRA. Yes, I've been given my notice.

MRS STOCKMANN. Your notice?

DR STOCKMANN. You too?

PETRA. Mrs Busk handed me my notice. I thought it was
better to leave immediately.

DR STOCKMANN. You did the right thing.

MRS STOCKMANN. Who'd have thought Mrs Busk was
that kind of person?

PETRA. Oh, Mother, Mrs Busk isn't like that really. She was
very uncomfortable about it. I could see that, but she didn't
dare do anything else, she said. So I had to leave.

DR STOCKMANN (*laughs and rubs his hands*). She didn't dare
do anything else – that's just marvellous!

MRS STOCKMANN. Well, after that disgraceful carry-on
last night, really…

PETRA. It wasn't *just* that. Wait till you hear this, Father!

DR STOCKMANN. Well?

PETRA. Mrs Busk showed me no fewer than three letters
she'd received this morning.

DR STOCKMANN. Anonymous, of course.

PETRA. Yes.

DR STOCKMANN. Yes, because they didn't dare sign their names, Katrine!

PETRA. And in two of them it said that a certain gentleman, a regular visitor to this house, had been talking to them in his club last night, and saying that I had some very radical opinions on all sorts of things.

DR STOCKMANN. I trust you didn't deny it?

PETRA. Indeed I didn't – you know me better than that. Actually, Mrs Busk has expressed some pretty radical opinions herself, from time to time, when we've been alone. But now that this has come out about me, she had no option but to let me go.

MRS STOCKMANN. And just think, this was from a regular visitor to the house. That's the thanks you get for your hospitality, Tomas!

DR STOCKMANN. Well, we won't have to live in this foul muck-heap for much longer. Pack up as quickly as you can, Katrine – let's get away from here, as far away as possible.

MRS STOCKMANN. Ssshh, Tomas – I think there's someone in the hall. See who it is, Petra.

PETRA (*opening the door*). Oh, Captain Horster, it's you. Please, do come in.

HORSTER (*from the hall*). Good morning. I thought I'd drop in just to see how you were doing.

DR STOCKMANN (*shakes his hand*). Thank you. That was very kind of you.

MRS STOCKMANN. And thanks for getting us home safely, Captain Horster.

PETRA. But how did you manage to get home yourself?

HORSTER. Oh, I managed. I'm pretty tough. And these people are mostly full of hot air.

DR STOCKMANN. Yes, well, that's no surprise, is it. Disgusting cowardice! Come here, I want to show you something. Look, these are all the stones they flung at us last night. Just look at that! Scarcely more than a couple of decent man-sized rocks in the whole pile – the rest are no better than pebbles, mere gravel. Standing out there bawling and shouting, swearing about how they were going to beat me up. But as for action, real action? No, there's precious little of that in this town.

HORSTER. It's just as well this time, doctor.

DR STOCKMANN. I suppose you're right. But it's galling all the same. If it should ever happen that this country finds itself in a real hand-to-hand scrap, you'll see how public opinion will be all for turning tail, and that solid majority, Captain Horster, will run for cover in the woods, like a flock of sheep. That's the really sad thing about all this, that's what upsets me – oh, the hell with it, who cares? It's so stupid, when you get right down to it. If they're saying I'm an enemy of the people, all right then, I'm an enemy of the people.

MRS STOCKMANN. That you could never be, Tomas.

DR STOCKMANN. Don't bank on it, Katrine. Being called a vile name works like being jabbed with a pin in the lung. And those damnable words… I can't get rid of them, they're lodged deep down in my heart, biting into me like acid. And there's no magnesia you can take for that, either.

PETRA. Oh, you should just laugh at them, Father.

HORSTER. They'll come to see things differently in time, doctor.

MRS STOCKMANN. They will, Tomas, as sure as you're standing here.

DR STOCKMANN. Yes, maybe, when it'll be too late. Well, it'll serve them right! And when they're sitting wallowing in their own filth, they'll be sorry they forced a genuine patriot to leave his native land. When does your ship sail, Captain Horster?

HORSTER. Hm – that's just what I've come to see you about.

DR STOCKMANN. Oh? Is there something wrong with the ship?

HORSTER. No – except that I won't be sailing with it.

PETRA. Don't tell me you've been given notice as well?

HORSTER. Yes, I'm afraid I have.

PETRA. You too?

MRS STOCKMANN. There you are, Tomas, you see?

DR STOCKMANN. And all for the sake of truth! Oh, if I'd thought for a moment that something like this would…

HORSTER. Oh, don't worry about it – I'll get a job with some other company away from here.

DR STOCKMANN. So much for our Mr Vik – a man of substance, dependent on nobody for anything. It's a damned shame!

HORSTER. He's actually quite reasonable otherwise. He said he'd like to have kept me on, but he didn't dare.

DR STOCKMANN. He didn't dare? No, that goes without saying.

HORSTER. It's not so easy, he said, when you belong to a party.

DR STOCKMANN. He never spoke a truer word, that fine friend of yours! A party's like a meat-grinder, it minces everyone's brains up to a kind of pulp, churning out a bunch of dolts and numskulls!

MRS STOCKMANN. Oh, Tomas!

PETRA (*to* HORSTER). If only you hadn't walked home with us, it might not have gone so far.

HORSTER. Well, I'm not sorry about it.

PETRA (*holds out her hand to him*). Thank you!

HORSTER (*to the* DOCTOR). Anyway, what I wanted to say was that if you're definitely set on leaving, I have another suggestion...

DR STOCKMANN. That's fine. Just as long as we can get away quickly.

MRS STOCKMANN. Ssshh! Listen, isn't that someone knocking?

PETRA. That'll surely be Uncle.

DR STOCKMANN. Aha! (*Calls.*) Come in!

MRS STOCKMANN. Now, Tomas dear, promise me...

The MAYOR *enters from the hall.*

MAYOR (*in the doorway*). Oh, you're busy, I see – I'd better...

DR STOCKMANN. No no – come in.

MAYOR. I'd rather we spoke in private.

MRS STOCKMANN. We'll go into the living room for the moment.

HORSTER. And I'll come back another time.

DR STOCKMANN. No, you go in with them, Captain Horster. I'd like to hear more about…

HORSTER. All right, I'll wait, then.

HORSTER *follows* MRS STOCKMANN *and* PETRA *into the living room. The* MAYOR *says nothing, but glances at the windows.*

DR STOCKMANN. It might be a bit draughty for you in here. Put your cap on.

MAYOR. Thank you. If you don't mind. (*Does so.*) I think I must've caught a cold yesterday – all that standing around, shivering.

DR STOCKMANN. Really? I was under the impression it was quite warm.

MAYOR. I'm sorry I wasn't able to prevent the excesses of last night.

DR STOCKMANN. Apart from that, have you anything in particular you want to say to me?

MAYOR (*takes out a large envelope*). I have this document for you – it's from the Baths Committee.

DR STOCKMANN. Notice to quit?

MAYOR. Yes, with effect from today. (*Lays the envelope on the table.*) This gives us no pleasure, but to be frank with you, we daren't do otherwise, given public opinion.

DR STOCKMANN. Daren't? I've heard that word somewhere before.

MAYOR. I'd like you to be quite clear about your position here. I'm afraid you can't rely on any sort of practice in the town for the foreseeable future.

DR STOCKMANN. The practice can go to hell! But what makes you so sure?

MAYOR. The Homeowners' Association is circulating a petition door-to-door, urging all responsible citizens to have nothing more to do with you. I'm pretty confident that not a single person will refuse to sign it. They simply wouldn't dare.

DR STOCKMANN. No, no – I don't doubt it. So?

MAYOR. If I might give you a piece of advice, it's that you should go away for a while.

DR STOCKMANN. Yes, I'd actually been thinking of leaving this town.

MAYOR. And after you'd had, say, six months or so to think things over – well, if after mature reflection, you felt able to pen a few words of apology, acknowledging your mistake…

DR STOCKMANN. I might possibly have my job back – is that what you were going to say?

MAYOR. Maybe. It's not altogether impossible.

DR STOCKMANN. Yes, but what about public opinion? I mean, you surely won't fly in the face of public opinion?

MAYOR. Opinion is an extremely volatile thing. And to be frank with you, it's a matter of considerable importance to us that we receive a written submission from you, to that effect.

DR STOCKMANN. Yes, I'm not surprised you've come sniffing around after that! Damn it to hell, man, have you forgotten what I've already said to you about these dirty tricks of yours?

MAYOR. Yes, well, you were in a different position then. You had the upper hand, with reason to believe that the whole town was behind you.

DR STOCKMANN. Yes, and now I'm being made to feel as if the whole town was on *top* of me! (*Flares up.*) Well, I don't care if the devil and his dam are on top of me, I won't do it! Never! Do you hear? Never!

MAYOR. A man with a family to support shouldn't be behaving the way you do, Tomas – you've no right.

DR STOCKMANN. I've no right, have I? Listen, there's only one thing on this earth that a free man daren't do – and do you know what that is?

MAYOR. No.

DR STOCKMANN. No, of course you don't. But I'll tell you. A free man dare not debase himself to behave like a wretch, he dare not sink so low as to feel like spitting in his own eye.

MAYOR. That's all well and good, if there weren't any other explanation for your pig-headedness – but in point of fact there *is* one.

DR STOCKMANN. What do you mean by that?

MAYOR. You know perfectly well what I mean. But speaking as your brother, and one who understands these things, I'd advise you not to place too much trust in certain expectations, or future prospects that might easily come to grief.

DR STOCKMANN. What on earth are you driving at?

MAYOR. Are you really asking me to believe that you're ignorant of the provisions of Morten Kiil's will?

DR STOCKMANN. As far as I know, what little he has is earmarked for an old folk's home. What's that got to do with me?

MAYOR. Well, in the first place, it's not so little. Morten Kiil is quite a wealthy man.

DR STOCKMANN. I had no idea.

MAYOR. Hm… Really? And I presume you had no idea either, that a substantial part of his fortune is to be left to your children? Furthermore, you and your wife are to receive the interest on that money during your lifetime. Didn't he ever tell you?

DR STOCKMANN. No, I'm damned if he did! On the contrary, he's done nothing but complain non-stop about the absurdly high taxes he has to pay. Are you quite sure about this, Peter?

MAYOR. Yes, I have it from a completely reliable source.

DR STOCKMANN. Well, thank God Katrine's future's secured – and the children's too! I must tell them! (*Calls out.*) Katrine! Katrine!

MAYOR (*holds him back*). Ssshh! Don't say anything yet.

MRS STOCKMANN (*opening the door*). What is it?

DR STOCKMANN. Nothing, dear. Just go back in again.

MRS STOCKMANN *does so.* DR STOCKMANN *paces the floor.*

Secure! Think of that – they're all secure, set up for life! It's a great feeling, to know that we're provided for!

MAYOR. Yes, but that's just the point – you're not secure. Kiil can alter his will any time he likes.

DR STOCKMANN. But he won't do that, my dear Peter. The old man's absolutely delighted at the way I've taken on you and your precious friends.

MAYOR (*starts, and looks intently at him*). Aha! That puts this business in an entirely different light.

DR STOCKMANN. What business?

MAYOR. The whole affair's been deliberately stage-managed. Wild accusations launched against the town's most prominent citizens – all in the name of truth, of course.

DR STOCKMANN. So? What about that?

MAYOR. It was nothing but a calculated ploy to get yourself named in Morten Kiil's will.

DR STOCKMANN (*almost speechless*). Peter – you're quite the most contemptible creature I've ever known – a true plebeian!

MAYOR. Be that as it may, we're finished – it's all over. Your dismissal notice is signed and sealed. And now we have a weapon to use against you. (*Goes out.*)

DR STOCKMANN. Well, of all the… (*Shouts.*) Katrine! I want this floor scrubbed clean! Tell that girl to bring a bucket of water – that one, what's her name, the one with the runny nose.

MRS STOCKMANN (*from the living room*). Ssshh! Not so loud, Tomas.

PETRA (*in the doorway*). Grandfather's here – he wants to know if he can have a word with you in private.

DR STOCKMANN. Yes, of course you can. (*At the door.*) Come in, Father-in-law.

MORTEN KIIL *enters. The* DOCTOR *closes the door after him.*

Now, what is it? Have a seat.

MORTEN KIIL. No, I won't sit down. (*Looks round the room.*) Very nice, Stockmann, I must say.

DR STOCKMANN. Yes, it is, isn't it.

MORTEN KIIL. Very nice indeed. Plenty of fresh air, too. All that oxygen you were talking about yesterday. You must have a pretty clear conscience today, I should think.

DR STOCKMANN. Yes, I have.

MORTEN KIIL. I fancied you would have. (*Pats his breast pocket.*) But can you guess what I've got in here?

DR STOCKMANN. A good conscience too, I hope.

MORTEN KIIL. Pah! Something better than that. (*Takes out a fat wallet, opens it, and shows him some papers.*)

DR STOCKMANN (*looks at him in astonishment*). You've bought shares in the Baths?

MORTEN KIIL. Yes. They weren't too difficult to get hold of today.

DR STOCKMANN. And you've gone out and bought…

MORTEN KIIL. As many as I could afford.

DR STOCKMANN. Father-in-law, dear – the way things are at the Baths just now…

MORTEN KIIL. Yes, but if you act sensibly, you'll soon have the Baths up and running again.

DR STOCKMANN. Yes, well, you can see for yourself, I've done all I could, but the people in this town are insane!

MORTEN KIIL. You were saying yesterday that the worst of the pollution came from my tannery. Well, if it's true, then my grandfather, my father before me, and myself – we must've been poisoning the town all these years, like three mass murderers – evil spirits. You don't think I can go on living here with the shame of that, do you?

DR STOCKMANN. Unfortunately, I'm afraid there's not much you can do about it.

MORTEN KIIL. Well… I value my good name too much. People call me the 'old Badger', so they tell me. And a badger's a sort of pig, isn't it? Yes, well, I'm never going to prove them right. I'll live and die a decent, honourable man.

DR STOCKMANN. And how will you manage that?

MORTEN KIIL. You're going to clear my name, Stockmann.

DR STOCKMANN. Me?

MORTEN KIIL. Have you any idea where I got the money from, to buy all these shares? No, how could you? Well, I'll tell you. This is the money that Katrine and Petra and the boys will inherit from me, because I've managed to put away a tidy sum, you know.

DR STOCKMANN (*flaring up*). You mean you've actually used Katrine's money for these?

MORTEN KIIL. Yes, I've invested the whole lot. And now I just want to see if you really are stark raving mad. Because if you're going to keep on about all the nasty beasts and suchlike coming out of my tannery, it'll be as if you're skinning Katrine alive, and Petra and the boys as well. And no decent father would do that, unless he's a madman.

DR STOCKMANN (*pacing up and down*). Yes, but I *am* a madman! I *am* a madman!

MORTEN KIIL. You couldn't be as stark raving mad as that, surely, when it affects your own wife and children?

DR STOCKMANN (*comes to a halt before him*). Why didn't you tell me what you were doing, before going out and buying up all this rubbish?

MORTEN KIIL. What's done is done, it can't be helped now.

DR STOCKMANN (*pacing the floor again*). I mean, if I wasn't so certain… But I'm convinced of it, I'm absolutely sure I'm in the right.

MORTEN KIIL (*weighing his wallet in his hand*). Well, if you keep on making these ridiculous claims, these things won't be worth much. (*Puts the wallet back in his pocket.*)

DR STOCKMANN. Damn it to hell, you'd think science could come up with some kind of prophylactic, some kind of preventative measure.

MORTEN KIIL. You mean something to kill off the beasts?

DR STOCKMANN. Yes, or render them harmless.

MORTEN KIIL. Couldn't you try a drop of rat poison?

DR STOCKMANN. Oh, don't talk nonsense! People keep telling me it's all in my imagination. All right, it's my imagination, let them have it their way! Those ignorant, narrow-minded mongrels had the cheek to call me an enemy of the people! And they were ready to rip my clothes off my back, too!

MORTEN KIIL. And they've smashed all your windows.

DR STOCKMANN. Yes, and harping on about my duty to my family. Well, I'll need to discuss that with Katrine – that's more in her line.

MORTEN KIIL. Good. Just mind you take her advice – she's a sensible woman.

DR STOCKMANN (*rounding on him*). And you're not exactly blameless either. How could you be so stupid, gambling away Katrine's money? You've put me in a terrible, painful dilemma. When I look at you now, it's as if I'm seeing the devil himself!

MORTEN KIIL. Anyway, I'd better go. But I expect to hear from you by two o'clock this afternoon. Yes or no. If the answer's no, the shares can go to charity. Today, mind, without fail.

DR STOCKMANN. And what will Katrine get then?

MORTEN KIIL. Not a penny.

The hall door opens. HOVSTAD *and* ASLAKSEN *are heard outside. They enter.*

Well, well, look who's here!

DR STOCKMANN (*glares at them*). What's this! You have the nerve to come into my home?

HOVSTAD. Yes, we have.

ASLAKSEN. Actually, we've got something to say to you.

MORTEN KIIL (*in a whisper*). Yes or no – by two o'clock.

ASLAKSEN (*with a glance at* HOVSTAD). Aha!

MORTEN KIIL *goes out.*

DR STOCKMANN. Well, what do you want with me? Make it quick.

HOVSTAD. Yes, I can well understand you feeling hostile towards us, after the position we adopted at yesterday's meeting.

DR STOCKMANN. You call that a position? Well, that was a pretty feeble position – absolutely spineless, like a pair of old women, God damn it!

ASLAKSEN. Call it whatever you please. There was nothing else we could do.

DR STOCKMANN. Nothing else you *dared* do, you mean!

HOVSTAD. If you like.

ASLAKSEN. Why didn't you drop us a hint beforehand? All it would have taken was a word to Mr Hovstad, or myself.

DR STOCKMANN. A hint? What about?

ASLAKSEN. About what lay behind it all.

DR STOCKMANN. I don't know what you're driving at.

ASLAKSEN (*nods knowingly*). Oh, I think you do, Dr Stockmann.

HOVSTAD. There's no need to keep it a secret any longer.

DR STOCKMANN (*looks from one to the other*). For God's sake, what *are* you on about!

ASLAKSEN. If I might enquire… hasn't your father-in-law been going round buying up all the shares in the Baths?

DR STOCKMANN. Yes, he's gone out and bought some today – so what?

ASLAKSEN. Well, it might have been cleverer if you'd got somebody else to do that – somebody not so closely related.

HOVSTAD. You shouldn't have done all this under your own name, either. I mean, nobody need have known that the attack on the Baths came from you. You should've let us in on it, Dr Stockmann.

DR STOCKMANN (*staring into space, the truth eventually dawning on him, he speaks as though thunderstruck*). This is unbelievable. Can this be possible?

ASLAKSEN (*smiles*). Obviously it can. But it ought to be done a little more subtly, you know.

HOVSTAD. And it's best to have a few other people in on it as well. That way, individual responsibility is limited.

DR STOCKMANN (*calmly*). Very well, gentlemen, come to the point. What is it you want?

ASLAKSEN. I think Mr Hovstad can best…

HOVSTAD. No, you go ahead, Aslaksen.

ASLAKSEN. Well, all right. Now that we can see how things stand, which way the wind blows, so to speak, we thought we might offer to put *The People's Courier* at your disposal.

DR STOCKMANN. You'd dare to do that? What about public opinion now? Aren't you afraid that that'll unleash a storm of protest?

HOVSTAD. We'll just have to weather the storm.

ASLAKSEN. And of course, you must be prepared to change your position quickly, doctor – once our campaign has achieved its goal.

DR STOCKMANN. You mean, as soon as my father-in-law and I have acquired these shares at a cut price?

HOVSTAD. Well, I presume it's mainly for research purposes that you want control of the Baths?

DR STOCKMANN. Of course. In fact, it was with a view to furthering my scientific research that I persuaded the old Badger to come in on it with me. So then we'll do some repairs to the pipes, dig up a bit of the beach, and it won't cost the town a penny. That'll do the trick, don't you think?

HOVSTAD. I would think so. As long as you've got the *Courier* on your side.

ASLAKSEN. In a free society, the press carries a great deal of weight, doctor.

DR STOCKMANN. Indeed it does. And so does public opinion. And you, Mr Aslaksen, will no doubt speak for the Homeowners' Association?

ASLAKSEN. Both the Homeowners' Association, and the Temperance Society, yes, you can count on that.

DR STOCKMANN. Actually, gentlemen, I feel a little embarrassed now, at having to ask this question – but what's in this for you?

HOVSTAD. Well, to tell you the truth, we'd rather take nothing at all for our help. However, the *Courier* is in a spot of bother at present, not doing too well. And I'd be very upset to see the paper go to the wall, especially now, when there are so many political issues to consider.

DR STOCKMANN. Yes, of course – that would be a bitter blow for someone like yourself, a friend of the people. (*Flares up.*) But I'm an *enemy* of the people! (*Pacing round the room.*) Where's my stick! Where the hell's my stick!

HOVSTAD. What *is* this?

ASLAKSEN. Surely you're not going to…?

DR STOCKMANN (*comes to a halt*). And supposing I don't give you a single penny from all my shares? We rich folk don't throw money away, you know. Just bear that in mind.

HOVSTAD. And *you* should bear in mind, doctor, that this business of the shares can be presented in two very different ways.

DR STOCKMANN. Yes, and you're the very man for the job. If I don't bail the *Courier* out, you'll take a jaundiced view of it all, you'll hunt me down, go for my throat, like a hound after a hare!

HOVSTAD. It's the law of nature, doctor – every animal needs must fight to survive.

ASLAKSEN. Yes, and take its food wherever it can find it, you know.

DR STOCKMANN. Well, let's just see if you can find anything out there in the gutter! (*Pacing round the room again.*) Because we're damn well going to find out which is the stronger animal among us three! (*Picks up his umbrella and brandishes it aloft.*) Now, watch out!

HOVSTAD. You wouldn't dare attack us!

ASLAKSEN. Watch what you're doing with that umbrella!

DR STOCKMANN. Right, Mr Hovstad – out the window with you!

HOVSTAD (*by the hall door*). Have you gone completely mad?

DR STOCKMANN. Out the window, Aslaksen – go on, jump! Quick as you like.

ASLAKSEN (*running round the table*). Moderation, my dear doctor! I'm not a well man. I can't stand this. (*Shouts.*) Help! Help!

MRS STOCKMANN, PETRA *and* CAPTAIN HORSTER *come running in from the living room.*

MRS STOCKMANN. Good God, Tomas – what on earth's going on?

DR STOCKMANN (*swinging his umbrella*). Jump, I'm telling you! Down into the gutter!

HOVSTAD. Attacking an innocent man! I'm calling you to witness this, Captain Horster! (*Hurrying out through the hall.*)

ASLAKSEN (*bewildered*). Anybody who knew what lay outside that window...! (*Slinks out through the living room.*)

MRS STOCKMANN (*hanging on to the* DOCTOR). Tomas, control yourself!

DR STOCKMANN (*throws his umbrella down*). Damn! I've let them get away!

MRS STOCKMANN. But what did they want with you?

DR STOCKMANN. I'll tell you later. I've got other things on my mind now. (*Goes over to the table and writes on a visiting card.*) Look, Katrine – d'you see what I've written?

MRS STOCKMANN. 'No', three times. What's that about?

DR STOCKMANN. I'll tell you that later too. (*Holds out the card.*) Here, Petra – give this to what's her name, sooty-face. Tell her to run over to the old Badger's with it, quick as she likes. Hurry!

PETRA *takes the card through to the hall.*

Yes, this has been some day for visitors – envoys from hell, or I don't know what. Well, now I'm going to sharpen my pen, skewer the lot of them. I'll dip it in venom and gall. I'll fire my inkpot straight at their skulls!

MRS STOCKMANN. Yes, Tomas, but aren't we leaving here?

PETRA *re-enters.*

DR STOCKMANN. Well?

PETRA. It's been sent.

DR STOCKMANN. Good! Leaving, did you say? No, I'm damned if we are! We're staying right where we are, Katrine.

PETRA. We're staying?

MRS STOCKMANN. In this town?

DR STOCKMANN. In this town, yes. That's where the battle is. This is where the fight will be fought, and where I'll triumph. As soon as I get my trousers stitched up, I'll go into town and look for lodgings somewhere. We need a roof over our heads for the winter.

HORSTER. You're welcome to stay at my place.

DR STOCKMANN. Can I?

HORSTER. Yes, of course you can. I've got plenty of room and I'm hardly ever at home.

MRS STOCKMANN. That's very kind of you, Captain Horster.

PETRA. Thank you!

DR STOCKMANN (*shakes his hand*). Thank you! Thank you! That's a load off my mind. Now I can get down to work in earnest. Oh, there's an endless stream of things that need investigating here, Katrine! It's just as well I can devote all my time to my researches now. Yes, because, well, you know, I've been given notice from the Baths...

MRS STOCKMANN (*sighs*). Yes, I was expecting that.

DR STOCKMANN. And they're going to take my practice away too. Well, let them. I'll keep the poor people anyway, the ones that never pay. And good heavens, they're the ones that need me most. But, by God, they're going to listen to what I've got to say. I'll preach to them, in season and out of season, as it says somewhere.

MRS STOCKMANN. But, Tomas dear, you've surely seen already that preaching to them doesn't do much good.

DR STOCKMANN. Now you're being silly, Katrine. D'you think I'm going to let public opinion, the solid majority, and all that infernal nonsense deflect me from my purpose? No, thanks! Besides, what I'm planning is quite simple and straightforward. I just want to get it into these mongrels' thick skulls that it's the so-called liberals that are the real enemies of the people, the real enemies of freedom! That the party programmes do nothing but choke the life out of every young and promising idea that comes their way; that political expediency is turning all our standards of morality and justice upside down, to the point that life's no longer worth living. I mean, Captain Horster, surely I can make them understand that much?

HORSTER. I suppose so. I know very little about these things myself.

DR STOCKMANN. Look, I'll tell you. It's the party bigwigs that need clearing out. A party leader is like a wolf, you see, a ravening grey wolf that needs to take so many victims each year to keep him going. Just look at Hovstad and Aslaksen. How many victims do you suppose they've devoured in their time? Either that or they've hurt them so badly, that they're fit for nothing except to sit on the town council and subscribe to the *Courier*! (*Sits on the edge of the table.*) Come over here, Katrine – look at the beautiful sunlight streaming in, the lovely, fresh springtime air along with it.

MRS STOCKMANN. Yes, Tomas – if only we could live on sunshine and fresh air!

DR STOCKMANN. Well, you'll have to scrimp and save a bit from here on in, Katrine. That's the least of my worries. No, the worst aspect of all this is that I don't know anybody with a free enough mind to carry on my life's work after me.

PETRA. Oh, don't even think about that, Father! You've got plenty of time… Look, the boys are home already.

EILIF *and* MORTEN *enter from the living room.*

MRS STOCKMANN. Have you got a holiday today?

MORTEN. No, but we got into a fight with some other boys at playtime.

EILIF. That's not true! They started it – they went for us.

MORTEN. And Mr Rørlund said it would be better if we stayed away a few days.

DR STOCKMANN (*snaps his fingers and jumps down from the table*). That's it! That's quite enough, by God! You're not setting foot in that school again!

THE BOYS. No more school!

MRS STOCKMANN. Oh, Tomas, really!

DR STOCKMANN. Never, I'm telling you! I'll teach you myself – which means you won't learn a blessed thing, but…

MORTEN. Hurrah!

DR STOCKMANN. I'll make free, independent men out of you. And you must help me, Petra.

PETRA. You can trust me, Father.

DR STOCKMANN. And we'll set up a school in the very room where they called me an enemy of the people. There aren't enough of us, though. I need twelve boys at least, to make a start.

MRS STOCKMANN. They're not going to be easy to find in this town.

DR STOCKMANN. We'll just have to see about that. (*To the* BOYS.) What about the boys on the streets – the real ragamuffins?

MORTEN. Yes, Father, I know lots of them!

DR STOCKMANN. So that's fine, then. Get hold of a couple of them for me. I'm going to experiment on these mongrels, just this once. Who knows what we might turn up amongst them?

MORTEN. But what are we going to do, when we've grown up into free and independent men?

DR STOCKMANN. Why, then you'll be able to drive all the ravening wolves out – out of the country!

EILIF *looks doubtful.* MORTEN *jumps for joy.*

MRS STOCKMANN. Let's just hope it's not the wolves that drive *you* out, Tomas.

DR STOCKMANN. Katrine, are you mad? Drive *me* out? When I'm the strongest man in the whole town?

MORTEN. Really?

DR STOCKMANN (*lowering his voice*). Ssshh! You mustn't say a word about it yet, but I've made a great discovery.

MRS STOCKMANN. What, again?

DR STOCKMANN. Yes, indeed I have! (*Gathers his family around him and speaks confidentially.*) The thing is, you see – the strongest man in the world is the man who stands alone.

MRS STOCKMANN (*smiles and shakes her head*). Oh, Tomas, Tomas…

PETRA (*bravely, grasping his hand*). Father!

Curtain.